Cambridge Elements

Elements in Writing in the Ancient World
edited by
Andréas Stauder
École Pratique des Hautes Études-PSL (EPHE)

HIERATIC

An Ancient Egyptian Cursive Script

Fredrik Hagen
University of Copenhagen

Shaftesbury Road, Cambridge CB2 8EA, United Kingdom

One Liberty Plaza, 20th Floor, New York, NY 10006, USA

477 Williamstown Road, Port Melbourne, VIC 3207, Australia

314–321, 3rd Floor, Plot 3, Splendor Forum, Jasola District Centre, New Delhi – 110025, India

103 Penang Road, #05-06/07, Visioncrest Commercial, Singapore 238467

Cambridge University Press is part of Cambridge University Press & Assessment, a department of the University of Cambridge.

We share the University's mission to contribute to society through the pursuit of education, learning and research at the highest international levels of excellence.

www.cambridge.org
Information on this title: www.cambridge.org/9781009673617

DOI: 10.1017/9781009673600

© Fredrik Hagen 2025

This publication is in copyright. Subject to statutory exception and to the provisions of relevant collective licensing agreements, no reproduction of any part may take place without the written permission of Cambridge University Press & Assessment.

When citing this work, please include a reference to the DOI 10.1017/9781009673600

First published 2025

A catalogue record for this publication is available from the British Library

ISBN 978-1-009-67365-5 Hardback
ISBN 978-1-009-67361-7 Paperback
ISSN 2753-6378 (online)
ISSN 2753-636X (print)

Cambridge University Press & Assessment has no responsibility for the persistence or accuracy of URLs for external or third-party internet websites referred to in this publication and does not guarantee that any content on such websites is, or will remain, accurate or appropriate.

For EU product safety concerns, contact us at Calle de José Abascal, 56, 1°, 28003 Madrid, Spain, or email eugpsr@cambridge.org

Hieratic

An Ancient Egyptian Cursive Script

Elements in Writing in the Ancient World

DOI: 10.1017/9781009673600
First published online: July 2025

Fredrik Hagen
University of Copenhagen
Author for correspondence: Fredrik Hagen, hagen@hum.ku.dk

Abstract: Hieratic was the most widely used script in ancient Egypt but is today relatively unknown outside Egyptology. Generally written with ink and a brush, it was the script of choice for most genres of text, in contrast to hieroglyphs, which were effectively a monumental script. The surviving papyri, ostraca, and writing boards attest to the central role of hieratic in Egyptian written culture and suggest that the majority of literate people were first (and not infrequently only) trained in the cursive script. This Element traces the long history of hieratic from its decipherment in the nineteenth century back to its origins around 2500 BC and explores its development over time, the different factors influencing its appearance, and the way it was taught and used.

Keywords: Egyptology, history of writing, archaeology, hieratic, scripts

© Fredrik Hagen 2025

ISBNs: 9781009673655 (HB), 9781009673617 (PB), 9781009673600 (OC)
ISSNs: 2753-6378 (online), 2753-636X (print)

Contents

1 Decipherment and History of Hieratic Studies	1
2 The Diachronic Development of the Script	5
3 Factors Governing the Visual Appearance of Hieratic	9
4 Uses	25
5 Scribal Training in Hieratic	51
6 Modern Research Tools	69
7 Publication Practices	72
8 Future Perspectives	78
References	81

Hieratic 1

1 Decipherment and History of Hieratic Studies

The script most commonly associated with ancient Egypt is hieroglyphs, a distinctive and visually complex script that had captured the imagination of both scholars and the public for hundreds of years even before its decipherment in the early nineteenth century. Yet for most of Egyptian history, this highly formal script was in effect monumental in nature (Vernus, 1990), existing not as the central script of written culture practised by the majority of literate individuals, but rather as a peripheral specialty of highly educated scribes. Alongside hieroglyphs there were cursive scripts that were used for most types of writing: for letters and administration, for literature, for rituals and prayers, for judicial texts, and for many other genres. The earliest of these cursive scripts was *hieratic*, which was used, in various contexts, from the Early Dynastic Period through to the Roman Period, so roughly from the early third millennium BCE to around the second or third century CE (Verhoeven, 2023a; Fischer-Elfert, 2021; Polis, 2020).[1]

The modern name *hieratic* comes from Greek descriptions of the script as *hieratiká grámmata* meaning 'sacred/priestly characters', attested in the second century CE in the writings of Clement of Alexandria. The label was no doubt derived from the use of the script at the time by Egyptian priests, who primarily employed it to write religious texts like rituals and funerary compositions (Fischer-Elfert, 2021: I, 4–5; Winand, 2020a: 166–168). By this stage hieratic had been replaced by other cursive scripts in everyday administration and communication, first by abnormal hieratic and then eventually by demotic, but not as a linear or abrupt historical development (Fischer-Elfert, 2021: II, 453–473; Donker van Heel, 2020: 593–595). Although the name 'hieratic' has stuck, it does not reflect the main areas of usage of the script for most periods of Egyptian history. In Egyptian the script is simply called 'writing' (*sḫ3*), with hieroglyphs referred to, at least in some periods, as 'divine words' (*mdw nṯr*; Allon, 2023); precisely how hieratic was conceptualised in its relation to hieroglyphs is a matter of debate, and may have changed over time, but the relatively distinct areas of usage – non-monumental versus monumental – would seem to signal a qualitatively different classification even in antiquity (e.g. Donnat Beauquier, 2014: 9–15, 194–207;

---

[1] The ancient dates used in this *Elements* volume are based on those given in the *Oxford History of Ancient Egypt* (Shaw, 2000), and are in every case approximations. This is also true when they are provided after the name of periods or dynasties: the New Kingdom has been rounded off to 'c. 1500–1000 BCE', rather than '1550–1069 BCE'. This has been done to simplify readers' chronological orientation, and I hope also to signal the uncertainty of many of the dates.

Ragazzoli and Albert, 2025: 32–37; but see Quack, 2010b: 236 for a slightly different view).

Originally the relationship between hieratic and hieroglyphs was quite close (Section 5.2): hieratic was essentially a cursive version of the hieroglyphic script with simplified forms that could be formed quickly with a reed brush and ink, and like the latter it was written mainly without punctuation (Section 4.4). Hieratic signs often look rather different from their original hieroglyphic counterparts, so that proficiency in one does not automatically mean that you can read the other. Today, students of Egyptology are normally taught to read hieroglyphs first, and then only later, if at all, do they work with cursive scripts such as hieratic and demotic. In antiquity this was the other way around: most literate individuals would have learned to read and write cursive scripts first, and then later – if at all – they would have specialised in hieroglyphs (Laboury, 2022: 61–66; cf. Section 5.1–3).

Awareness in Europe of hieratic as an ancient Egyptian cursive script has its roots in the late seventeenth century, but knowledge of its existence was distinctly limited at that point (Aufrère, 2009: 32–35). A French consul, Benoit de Maillet, had brought back as early as 1698 a hieratic *Book of the Dead* on linen from a Saqqara tomb (Louvre N 3059), which he had presented at the royal court of Louis XIV, apparently arousing significant interest. He wrote to a colleague that 'Here is incontrovertible proof that the ancient Egyptians, contrary to the universally held opinion, had a script in which to express themselves, different from the hieroglyphic script … a rarer and more ancient manuscript than those found in any library of the world' (Ormont, 1902: I, 284; translated from the French by the author). Other manuscripts followed, and although this mysterious script occasionally appeared in the scientific literature – and on one memorable occasion was even incorporated into a splendid work of art given to Augustus II of Poland, Saxonia, and Lithuania in 1738 (Fischer-Elfert, 2021: I, 20–21; Lüscher, 2017: 369), it was not until the work of Jean-François Champollion that things really progressed. Before him the general opinion, with some notable exceptions like Thomas Young, was that the cursive hieratic script was essentially an alphabet that only represented sounds and which might be compared to ancient Semitic scripts, or even Chinese, unlike the hieroglyphic script which was seen as heavily symbolic (Winand, 2021: 297–298).

The history of the decipherment of hieratic is inextricably linked to that of hieroglyphs, and in fact proceeded alongside it (Polis, 2020: 552–553). In 1815 Young confirmed that there was a direct link between the two scripts, based on a comparison of sections of *Book of the Dead* manuscripts in (cursive) hieroglyphs and hieratic, identified by their use of identical vignettes (Buchwald & Josefowicz, 2022: 264, 276, 421). Six years later, Champollion published his *De l'écriture hiératique des anciens Égyptiens* (1821), and in his famous *Précis du système hiéroglyphique des anciens Égyptiens*, published some three years later and described as 'the decisive step in decipherment' (Parkinson, 1999: 38), the hieratic script was also an important component (Buchwald & Josefowicz, 2022: 321, 335). In that work Champollion included palaeographical tables of hieroglyphic signs with their hieratic counterparts that he had collected (Posener, 1972; see Figure 1 for an example from his unpublished notes), which are not dissimilar to the main palaeographical tools used today (Section 6.2). In addition to the decipherment of hieroglyphs, Champollion's main methodological contributions to hieratic was to confirm that the hieratic script was directly derived from hieroglyphs and that one could therefore establish a one-to-one correspondence between individual signs in both scripts (as had already been suggested by Young), and – eventually – to show that the system as a whole functioned precisely the same way, with both phonographic signs, logograms, and determinatives (or classifiers).

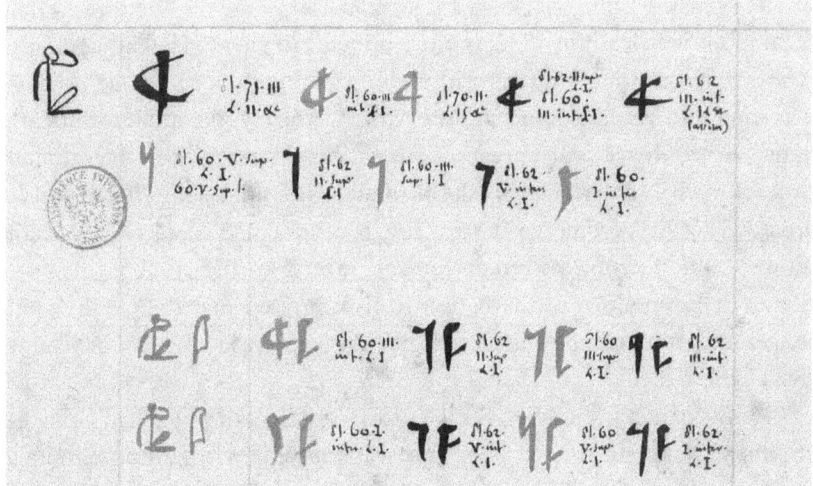

Figure 1 A page from Champollion's papers showing him collecting examples of hieratic signs from different manuscripts, ordered according to the corresponding hieroglyph, in a manner reminiscent of modern palaeographical tables. The hieratic examples of 𓎛 notably include both the full and the abbreviated forms. Papiers de J.-Fr. Champollion le jeune, XIXᵉ siècle. 1ʳᵉ série. IX–X Notes sur l'écriture hiératique, NAF 20311, 126. Copyright Bibliothèque Nationale de France.

In addition to his work deciphering the scripts, Champollion also made a number of important historical discoveries, both in France and in Egypt. One example that demonstrates his remarkable hieratic skills became evident on his return from Egypt in 1830 when he made a stop in Aix-en-Provence on his way to Paris. While in Egypt he had seen, among many other monuments, the great reliefs telling the story of the Battle of Kadesh from the reign of Ramesses II; these are inscribed on temple walls in hieroglyphs, with accompanying scenes showing the pharaoh and various episodes from the battle. Back in France he discovered that one of the papyri in the famous collection of François Sallier contained a narrative of the very same historical event, albeit in a distinctly literary form (Fischer-Elfert, 2021: I, 34–35). The papyrus is now in the British Museum (Figure 6) and contains the composition known in Egyptological literature as 'The Kadesh Poem' or 'The Poem of Pentaour', from Champollion's original labelling of it as a *poème*. To have recognised that these two sources contained the same text is impressive, because there is nothing but the actual text of the hieratic manuscript to go on: if one cannot transcribe and (at least in part) read it, it is not possible to link it to the scenes and hieroglyphic texts on the temple walls.

The general state of knowledge, especially in the decades after Champollion's death in 1832, is more difficult to gauge. He had certainly made a breakthrough, but as with most scientific discoveries the process was long and complex, and the real world is rarely like a code-cracking game. Not only were there several other scholars involved in the original process, such as Johan David Åkerblad and Thomas Young (Buchwald & Josefowicz, 2022), but the breakthrough represented a start more than an end. Many problems remained, and several of the great intellectual figures in Egyptology of the period freely admitted that to actually read longer and more complex ancient Egyptian texts was still a real challenge (Schenkel, 2012).

In terms of hieratic studies, the year 1890 represents a watershed moment (Fischer-Elfert, 2021: I, 45–48). This was the year when Adolf Erman's fundamental study of Papyrus Westcar (P. Berlin 3033) appeared, a hieratic manuscript containing what is today one of the most famous literary narratives from ancient Egypt, *King Kheops and the Magicians* (Blackman, 1988; Lepper, 2008). In this two-volume work Erman demonstrated two approaches to dating Egyptian texts and manuscripts that were to have a profound methodological influence on the field. In the first volume he analysed the language of the composition, making a distinction between older (Middle Egyptian) and more recent (Late Egyptian) language stages, and, significantly, found grammatical elements of both in the same text – in effect the first attempt in Egyptology at linguistic dating. In the second volume he systematically collected palaeographical data, not just from the Berlin papyrus but also from other manuscripts, and ordered and classified them to show how the hieratic script developed, using this model to place the production of Papyrus Westcar at a specific point in time. As with the linguistic dating, his palaeographical model enabled him to suggest a plausible date for the copying of the manuscript. He was also one of first to remark on the difference between a rather cursive business-style and a more uncial literary style of hieratic. It is difficult to overstate the importance of Erman's achievements for hieratic studies, and the general principles which he laid out are essentially the same as those followed by modern editors of hieratic texts (see also Section 6.2 for his student Georg Möller and his continuation and development of Erman's work).

2 The Diachronic Development of the Script

The question of when hieratic became a separate script distinct from hieroglyphs is largely a matter of definition (Fischer-Elfert, 2021: I, 6–7, 55–61). Early texts written with ink display a tendency to simplify signs, becoming more and more cursive, but it was a gradual process. Although the early evidence is limited, it seems likely that a simplified script, used perhaps primarily for administrative purposes, developed shortly after the emergence of the hieroglyphic script. Most scholars put the final stage of this initial process, that is to say the point at which one can safely talk about hieratic forms of signs, at the end of the 2nd Dynasty, or around 2700 BCE (Regulski, 2009, 2010). From this point forward hieratic remained the most commonly used script for about 2,000 years, until the emergence of demotic in the middle of the seventh century BCE. It did not disappear entirely, however, and as mentioned earlier it was later mainly used to write religious texts in temples.

The development of hieratic from the beginning of the script until its gradual disappearance in the second and third centuries CE can be reconstructed in broad terms which allow for a rough palaeographic dating of individual manuscripts (Section 3.1). There is not yet an established terminology or even criteria for its stages of development (Verhoeven, 2015: 47–48), and the following schematic presentation makes no claim to reflect the ancient evidence other than very broadly. In brief the oldest stage of hieratic (c. 2700–2100 BCE) is characterised by forms that reflect the original hieroglyphs to a greater extent than later periods, with clear spacing of signs and few ligatures. A middle stage (c. 2100–1600 BCE) has a stronger tendency to use ligatures and also sees – on current evidence – the first distinction between a specific style used in literary versus administrative contexts (Section 3.3). This is also the time when the layout of most texts changes from a vertical format (columns) to a horizontal one (lines), which probably happened around 1800 BCE (Section 4.4). The hieratic of the Second Intermediate Period and the New Kingdom (c. 1600–1000 BCE) continues these trends in several ways: the two different registers or styles continue to develop, with the administrative one using more ligatures and abbreviations, while the literary one is more detailed, with most signs clearly written. At the end of the New Kingdom and for the few next centuries (c. 1000–800 BCE), administrative hieratic became so abbreviated and cursive that it often poses serious challenges for modern editors to decipher (Figure 3; Fischer-Elfert, 2021: II, 433–441). From this process there emerged two distinct traditions, in Upper and Lower Egypt, which Egyptologists call respectively abnormal hieratic (c. 700–550 BCE) and demotic (c. 650 BCE–400 CE). The precise chronology and mechanisms of this development is still being mapped, but the result is clear: by the mid-sixth century BCE demotic had replaced abnormal hieratic, including in the south, and was finally adopted as the everyday script by the whole country (Donker van Heel, 2020). This was not the end of the more literary form of hieratic (*Buchschrift*) by any means, but it was gradually restricted in use until ultimately only priests were required to learn it. As Stadler (2008: 167) points out, the restriction in this use of hieratic to write literary and religious texts in temples broadly correlates to the emergence of demotic, which takes over the previous role of hieratic.

Like its origins, the end of hieratic is difficult to pin down, partly because a number of Roman Period manuscripts remain to be published, and partly because this late phase of the script has not yet been systematically studied (Quack, 2015, 2017a). The somewhat simplified narrative of its history – from an early status as an everyday script to one that was later employed primarily in temple contexts – is broadly true, but even as late as the first and second centuries CE there are examples of letters written in the hieratic script but with mainly demotic language, including a use of the ancient letter formula 'It is good that you listen' (*nfr sḏm=k*; Quack, 2019, 2020b). Knowledge of hieratic was restricted to priestly communities by then, which suggests that these documents stem from that social context and more specifically from highly educated priests (one writer was a 'scribe of the book'). Beyond such exceptional cases, it is clear that hieratic towards the end of its existence was used mainly for older religious compositions, and that the final decline of the script is inextricably linked to the disappearance of contexts in which such texts were relevant (Stadler, 2008). In practice this constitutes temples as sites for active cults honouring Egyptian deities in the traditional manner using rituals transmitted in papyrus manuscripts, as well as tombs, where *The Book of the Dead*, *Books of Breathing*, and similar compositions were no longer included as part of the funerary equipment of the deceased. This gradual phasing out of hieratic in the second and third centuries CE can be seen in a few securely dated manuscripts – a *Book of the Fayum* is dated to year 20 of the emperor Hadrian (135 CE), for example, and there are hieratic mummy labels from the early third century too (Quack, 2016a) – but in general the final phase is not well documented (Fischer-Elfert, 2021: II, 555–610). The gradual switch to (Old) Coptic, whose emergence can be traced in the use of the script to gloss demotic and hieratic texts in temple settings, had probably replaced the traditional scripts almost entirely by the late third century CE (Quack, 2017b). It is not possible to identify the last surviving hieratic document with any certainty, but a plausible candidate was suggested by Fischer-Elfert (2021: II, 608). This is a magical text (P. BM EA 10588) from the third century CE,[2] which has an incantation for providing a divine answer in a dream. In the instructions for the spell, there is a list of seven forms of Thoth and Horus whose names should be written on a laurel leaf and placed under one's head when resting, but unlike the spell itself, which is in demotic, the four first beings are written in Greek, and the next three are written in hieratic: a falcon (*bik*), baboon (*ꜥny*), and ibis (*ḥb*), with hieroglyph-like determinatives. Here, as so often in the very last stages of the script, hieratic is mixed with others, but the author was clearly someone conversant with demotic as well, writing both with a steady and practised hand.

Even in such a broad history of the script, many details remain uncertain and unclear. This is partly due to the rare and uneven survival of the material, but is also due to our limited understanding of the process of acquisition of literacy (Section 5), and the degree to which this process was governed by, and responded to, historical circumstances. To what extent the forms of the script and its orthography was consciously revised and updated has not been studied systematically, and yet one of

---

[2] The precise date is debated: the original editors suggested late third century CE (Bell, Nock & Thompson, 1933: 5–6) based on the Greek text, but admitted that 'the hand ... is not very easy to date at all closely', while Quack (2022: 54 n. 126) suggested 'early or mid' third century. Whether or not it is the very last example identified so far, it is certainly from the final phase of hieratic.

the most striking aspects of Egyptian written culture is its homogeneity in appearance, orthography, and use of formulas. That is not to say that everything is entirely standardised, and philologists have seized on minor variations in their search for dialects, regional variation in spellings, and so on, but the implication of this homogeneity itself has been less explored. The exception is when standardisation slips a little, and here recent research on the transitional period from hieratic to abnormal hieratic and demotic has suggested that whereas the first shows signs of an 'organic development' with many 'varied ways of writing particular words', the latter has the hallmarks of 'a conscious and standardized writing system' in terms of orthography and formulas, which can be linked to the political situation of a ruler in the north (Psammetik I) gradually consolidating power over a newly reunited country (Donker van Heel, 2020: 593–594). Egyptian history includes several periods characterised by a collapse of the central power of kingship, when the art, architecture, and even language of elite culture changed significantly, followed by periods of re-unification when there is a distinctive return to older styles – the early 18th Dynasty (c. 1550–1400 BCE) and its focus on Middle Kingdom (c. 2000–1650 BCE) traditions is one of the most famous examples (Kahl, 2010: 5–6). It might be possible to trace comparable developments in hieratic, if sufficient data comes to light, but so far there is only limited evidence for this. Megally (1971: 1–15, 52) suggested that there was a more or less systematic revision, particularly of administrative hieratic forms, in the early 18th Dynasty, whereby signs were more closely modelled on their hieroglyphic counterparts rather than adapted from the already extremely cursive Middle Kingdom administrative hieratic (cf. Parkinson & Quirke, 1995: 27). Anyone who has worked with documents from these two periods will readily concur with the observation that the more recent ones are definitely less cursive in their forms and more restrained in their uses of ligatures than the older ones. The implication might be that political history influenced the standardisation of hieratic, which is an intriguing thought. Some caution may be in order, however, because the number of manuscripts that can be safely dated to this transitional period is not great, and with low numbers one runs the risk of confusing personal or even local styles with broader tendencies. It might be worth exploring the political aspects of the development of hieratic further in the future, and there have been studies of potentially comparable phenomena elsewhere in the writing system. An analysis of changes over time in the way determinatives or classifiers were used in hieroglyphic inscriptions, for example, suggested that there was a reorganisation of the system in the second half of the reign of Ramesses II, which broadly speaking seems to match the development of linguistic stages of Late Egyptian (both script and vocalisation; Chantrain, 2014). This in turn was thought to imply state agency behind it (Chantrain, 2021), but the data is patchy, and the development is at least partly gradual rather than a sudden revision; it can hardly be considered more than a hypothesis at this stage. Some Second Intermediate Period (c. 1650–1550 BCE) texts in hieratic, as an example of manuscripts from a period without a unifying nationwide state apparatus, can be difficult to read precisely because they display unfamiliar features, such as signs overlapping each other, and a tendency for horizontal flourishes to be added to vertical signs, but whether this is a chronological feature or an aspect of personal style is not clear (Hagen, 2019a: 205; for overlapping signs as a personal style in one Ramesside hand, see Polis, 2022: 414 n. 34). However, there are long and well-preserved manuscripts from the same period that are much easier to read (Fischer-Elfert, 2021: 297–300). There are also examples where developments looked backwards in time, similar to the archaism that has been observed in art history and linguistics. Sometime in the 22nd Dynasty (c. 950–700 BCE), for example, there was a return to older forms for some hieratic signs (Verhoeven, 2001: 250–256), in effect a kind of visual archaism that can complicate efforts to date a manuscript: the writing board with the *Tale of Neferkare and General Sisenet* (Chicago OIM 13539), for example, was originally thought to be from the late 18th or early 19th Dynasty (c. 1300 BCE; Posener, 1957), but was recently redated to the 22nd–26th Dynasties (c. 950–550 BCE) due to the recognition of the archaism at work (Quack, 2022: 95). Such examples show that the long history of hieratic is not one of a simple linear development from less to more cursive forms, but the mechanisms of change are obscure, and we are often left wondering if what we see are traces of gradual and natural developments or more sudden and formally instigated reforms.

3 Factors Governing the Visual Appearance of Hieratic

As a cursive script, the appearance of hieratic is extremely varied due to a range of factors: the date of the manuscript, the writing materials used (brush/pen and ink, or scratched into rock), the care of the copyist and the choice of graphic register or style (calligraphic book manuscript, or a shopping list), geographical origins of the scribe (where was he trained?), and, of course, the peculiarities of an individual's personal handwriting. This is not an exhaustive or a hierarchical list, but it exemplifies some of the areas that researchers have grappled with in the study of hieratic.

3.1 Date

During its long existence hieratic was continually developing, and its visual appearance has frequently been a key factor when scholars have attempted to date manuscripts. In palaeographical studies it is common to refer to its various stages by labels such as 'Middle Kingdom hieratic', 'New Kingdom hieratic', and 'Roman Period hieratic', and although each has certain characteristics that are, to an extent, recognisable by specialists, it is often difficult to be exact beyond this broad dating. This problem is particularly acute because palaeographical dating is not infrequently one of the main dating tools available: the majority of papyrus manuscripts lack an archaeological context that might help date them, even if – in the case of non-literary texts at least – onomastics and prosopography, as well as grammar and lexicography, can be indicative of specific sites and periods. Stylistic criteria of the hieratic script can be used to suggest a historical period of origin, and lists of diagnostic signs, based on documents whose dating can be independently verified by other means, were first drawn up for comparison with unprovenanced and undated manuscripts over a hundred years ago (Möller, 1920; but cf. Megally, 1971: xix, n. 2). Although the basic premise of assigning a date based on developments in the script is generally accepted, there are significant methodological challenges facing research into the use of palaeographical methods to establish narrower dates (Fischer-Elfert, 2021: II, 355). The most problematic is the rare and uneven survival of manuscripts, both chronologically and geographically (Section 3.4).

The gradual development of the script was mapped by Georg Möller (1927–36), and subsequent analyses of specific periods (Regulski, 2010; Verhoeven, 2001; Wimmer, 1995; Goedicke, 1988) or corpora (Edel, 1980) have done much to improve our understanding of its changes over time, as have many editions of individual papyri which also include palaeographical data. All of this is now being analysed and made accessible online by the *Altägyptische Kursivschriften* (AKU) project by the Academy of Sciences and Literature in Mainz (Gülden, 2023a, 2023b; Gülden, Krause, & Verhoeven, 2020). One of its core contributions is an updated online database of sign forms (https://aku-pal.uni-mainz.de/) and associated metadata that enables the material to be sorted by date, media (papyrus; ostraca; writing boards; graffiti; etc.), findspot, and – crucially – genre. This addresses one of the key weaknesses of previous resources, which posed serious methodological challenges for those seeking to date texts by palaeographical criteria. To take just two examples, Möller's standard work (1927–36) was criticised for focusing mainly, but by no means exclusively, on literary manuscripts, which made it difficult to use for those working with administrative documents, and although Wimmer's analysis (1995) of exclusively administrative ostraca was a definite step forward, it was also challenged on several points, with Jac. Janssen, one of the most prominent specialists in the field, expressing his 'scepticism regarding the possibilities of dating a hieratic text, other than very roughly, on the basis of individual signs' (Janssen, 1987: 161; but cf. also Wimmer, 2001: 286). Janssen himself went on to say that 'Everyone dealing with ostraca is after some time able to distinguish, in most cases, between 19th- and 20th-Dynasty texts, without being capable of exactly saying on which criteria he bases his intuitive feeling' (Janssen, 1997: 339), but his caution is worth keeping in mind. There are cases where palaeographical dating has been problematic, to say the least: for example, a late 11th-Dynasty (c. 2000 BCE) dish from Elephantine with a note concerning payment for rights to a tomb was mistakenly assigned a date almost 200 years too early, before the typology of the object was eventually taken into account (Fischer-Elfert, 2021: I, 149–151, 185, and cf. 251–255). Such examples are luckily not common, but neither are they as rare as one might wish. Future work will undoubtedly refine the criteria available, and it is worth noting that a recent attempt at applying Wimmer's dating criteria to literary texts which can be dated on other grounds was broadly successful (Dorn, 2022).

Even when an absolute date for a document can be established by other means, for example if it bears a regnal date, it can be informative to look at variations in the hieratic script(s). An interesting text that showcases some of the methodological problems involved is the so-called *Saite Oracular Papyrus* (P. Brooklyn 47.218.3), a document dated to 651 BCE. This is a curious papyrus, the interpretation of which is not entirely clear: the most common view is that concerns a priest who is asking the god of his temple, on behalf of his father, whether the latter may be transferred to a different temple. It is unlikely to be a regular administrative document, however: with an elaborate vignette featuring the priests of the temple carrying the divine image of Amun-Re at the beginning, including a series of named high-ranking priests facing them, it is an elaborate and stylised record, written in a particularly formal hieratic hand. Unusually, the actual record of the event occupies only a single column, whereas the following eighteen columns have a long list of witness signatures by fifty individuals who represent the great and the good of the priestly milieu of Thebes at this time. What is interesting is that of these witnesses, seventeen write in (literary) hieratic, twenty-seven write in abnormal hieratic, and the remaining six use a mixture of the two (Parker, 1962: 14–34). This has been analysed in view of the assumed levels of training and family history of the priests (Helck, 1984), but it is also worth noting that the hieratic used is not homogenous in style between the different writers, which has consequences for the precision of the dating methodology. The observations of Verhoeven (2001: 59–60) are pertinent here: she noted that there are differences between types of priests, where those whose actual duties involved the reading and copying of hieratic manuscripts display a more consistent and calligraphic style, but she also suggested that the style of writing might be influenced by the age of the writer, much like a modern family might have parents who write in cursive while the next generation prefers block letters – one Egyptian scribe may be using a more old-fashioned style than his apprentice, even if they are active at the same point in time (cf. Fischer-Elfert, 2021: I, 227; II, 417 n. 40; Janssen, 1997: 343). In other words, although the availability of more data should enable future work to calibrate existing models, there is a natural limit to how specific such dating can be.

3.2 Writing Materials

As a cursive script, hieratic was mainly written using ink and a brush or pen, with the scribe sitting cross-legged, either on the ground or perhaps on a low bench, with a papyrus or writing board across the knees. Holding the brush in the right hand at a short distance from the writing surface, he would use the left to balance the writing board or to hold the papyrus taut, and write from right to left, replenishing the ink at intervals. The dipping of the pen consisted of moistening it in a small pot of liquid and then swirling it on a cake of black or red ink. This liquid may not always have been purely water, as the ink might need some form of protein to acquire the pigment density observed in some of the ancient papyri (T. Christiansen, personal communication).

The appearance of hieratic naturally changes according to the tools and media that are employed, even if the basic sequence of strokes might be similar. This is obvious when comparing, for example, rock-carved graffiti with papyrus manuscripts bearing a text written in ink (Dorn, 2015), but there is variation in technology also within the latter group that affects its appearance. The reed brush, dipped in ink, was used from the earliest times, and this had a tip that was crushed in order to create a soft head. This meant that it responded to differences in angle and pressure to produce lines of varying width, creating easily recognisable organic curves that to the untrained eye might be reminiscent of Chinese or Arabic calligraphy.

The introduction of the reed pen (*calamus*) in the late second century BCE (Quack, 2015: 444–445) changed the appearance of hieratic texts considerably: this instrument consisted of a hollow reed sharpened into a hard tip that produced a line of uniform width, more like a modern pencil, without the flowing strokes that characterised the earlier periods (Figure 2).

A standard scribal palette consisted of a wooden container for reed brushes, with one black and one red ink pad embedded in the surface. Black was used most frequently, with red normally reserved for specific parts of a text (e.g. headings, rubrics, corrections and versepoints; cf. Section 4.4). There are no ancient Egyptian descriptions of ink manufacturing (Christiansen, 2017), and scientific analysis of Egyptian ink is still in its infancy (Christiansen et al., 2020), but a simple carbon-based ink, consisting of soot mixed with water and gum arabic, seems to have been in use since at least the late Predynastic (c. 3200 BCE). At some point before the third century BCE so-called mixed ink was introduced, which incorporated traces of metals such as copper, iron, or lead. To what extent variations in manufacture would affect the appearance of the ink, such as the use of different types of soot, for example, is not known (see Polis, 2022: 409, for an example where an odd variation in ink density seems typical of a specific scribe) but it might affect the density of the colour and its resistance to environmental factors such as sunlight, and it is possible that the quality of ink might affect how often the brush would need to be dipped (cf. Brawanski, 2019: 153, on red ink needing more frequent dipping).

Figure 2 Roman Period hieratic written with a reed brush (a; P. Carlsberg 1) and a reed pen (b; P. Carlsberg 312). The brush produced strokes that vary greatly in line width, as shown in how the diagonal strokes taper to a very thin line towards the bottom left, while the pen (*calamus*) produced strokes with a more consistent line width.
Courtesy of the Papyrus Carlsberg Collection, Copenhagen.

It has been shown for the Tebtunis temple library (c. 200 BCE–200 CE) that a scribe could use different inks on different manuscripts, and even several inks on a single papyrus roll (Christiansen et al., 2017: 219), but this may be a consequence of the complex logistics of the system – production, distribution, and access – rather than a deliberate choice by the scribe.

3.3 Graphic Registers and Styles

It has long been accepted that at least from the Middle Kingdom (c. 2000–1600 BCE) onwards there is a notable difference in the appearance of the hieratic that was used to write administrative and literary texts (Fischer-Elfert, 2021: I, 222). Literary hieratic is characterised by clearly formed individual signs and fewer ligatures, often quite tall writing, and a deliberate, almost calligraphic, style. Administrative hands tend to be more rapid, with smaller signs and rather abbreviated forms, more ligatures, and a distinctly cursive appearance (Verhoeven, 2023a: 1; Fischer-Elfert, 2020: 658). Specialists regularly label texts as written in a 'literary hand' ('uncial' or 'book-hand') or 'administrative hand' ('business hand' or 'short hand'), and even if this is often done intuitively rather than as a result of applying a set of objective criteria, few have quibbled with the categories. Recently, however, this division has been questioned (Moezel, 2022: 11; Polis, 2022: 441; for similar concerns in Greek and Latin papyrology, see Cavallo, 2011: 101–102), and the debate is far from settled. As further research is carried out a more nuanced picture emerges, and it should be kept in mind that we are dealing with a (once) living tradition that consequently embodies the full range of variations and idiosyncrasies that is to be expected when human beings are involved. Common sense dictates that graphic register, whether 'literary' and 'administrative' styles exist as absolute categories or not, is partly a matter of personal choice on behalf of the scribe: any individual would have had a range of different registers at their disposal, from the most rapid and cursive, in extreme instances legible perhaps mainly to themselves, to an extravagant and careful hand for those cases where legibility to others (and perhaps aesthetic appearance) was a major concern. The choice of graphic register could be influenced by many factors and was not only a matter of personal preference: social context was important, and a writer might be swayed by the expectations of the literary tradition, or by superiors concerned with the legibility of a document. A study of the handwriting of the scribe Amennakht (active c. 1200–1150 BCE; cf. Section 3.5) suggested that the degree of 'sacrality' of the text being copied was a factor in choice of register, with observable differences in his literary register between hymns, a praise of cities poem, and a satirical text (Dorn & Polis, 2017: 73). In late Old Kingdom Balat (c. 2500–2200 BCE), letters sent to the governors' palace from surrounding villages display a style that is characterised by large signs, clearly separated, with few ligatures, while documents written in the palace itself have smaller and more cursive signs, with less deeply carved lines (Pantalacci, 2018: 225). Importantly, this need not be an either-or situation where each text or document is written exclusively in one style or the other. Old Kingdom (c. 2600–2100 BCE) texts can have opening lines with the royal titulary in hieroglyphs followed by cursive hieratic (Fischer-Elfert, 2021: I, 71), and in the Ramesside Period (c. 1300–1000 BCE) it seems to have been common in official administrative documents to write the first few lines, often containing date formulas and royal titularies, with larger and more calligraphic signs sometimes referred to as 'chancery script' (*Kanzleischrift*), before resuming a more normal administrative hieratic style (Demarée, 2018: 277–278; compare Roman period examples of imperial titularies in hieratic, followed by cursive demotic notes; Ryholt, 2020b). This switching between graphic registers can also be used to create structure in longer administrative documents, as in a list of fields (c. 1000 BCE) belonging to various high-ranking individuals and institutions (Figure 3), where the first line, giving the identity of the owner of the fields, is in large and calligraphic writing, followed by several lines in what Gardiner called 'the minutest cursive hieratic I have ever seen', full of abbreviations (Gardiner, 1941: 65; cf. Fischer-Elfert, 2020: 649; Gasse, 1988: I, 5–6, pls. 1–2).

In terms of modern accessibility the headings are legible to most hieratic students, while the extremely cursive writing used for the body of the text is challenging even for specialists (Haring, 1997: 326–340; Vleeming, 1991). The difference in appearance is clearly due to a deliberate switch in registers, but the scribe seems to have used a different (thinner) brush for the more cursive lines, which, along with the use of many abbreviations, would have affected the speed of writing (Fischer-Elfert, 2021: II, 436). Letters could also be written in a more or less formal style depending on the nature of the message and the relationship of the writer to the addressee, but even within a single letter the style can change from opening lines in larger and more carefully written signs, with widely spaced lines, to a more cursive style with a more compact structure in the body of the text (Figure 4). Such examples showcase the ability of scribes to switch between registers at will (see also Dorn, 2015 on the scribe Amennakht; and cf. Section 3.5).

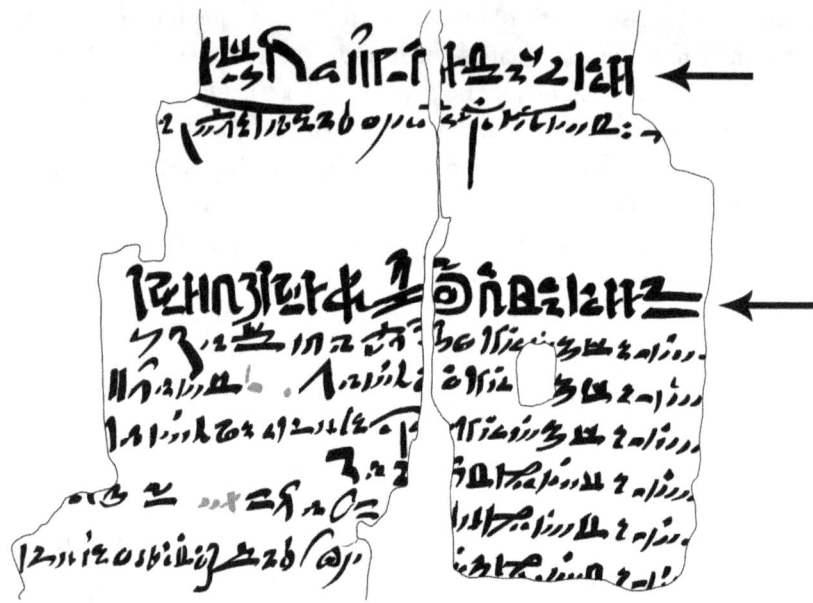

Figure 3 Facsimile drawing of part of P. Louvre AF 6345 (col. II), showing a list of fields belonging to two institutions which owed tax payments, one being the 'Palanquin of the High Priest of Amun', the other the 'Temple of Ramesses III in the Estate of Amun'. The arrows highlight the headings written in a more uncial or 'literary' hieratic than the body of the text, which illustrates a scribe switching hieratic registers as he went along. Drawing by F. Hagen.

To some extent the style of hieratic seems to have been influenced by types of genre beyond the traditional – although by no means universal – distinction between administrative and literary texts. In addition to the example of the scribe Amennakhte cited earlier, an extreme case is the composition known as *Kemit* ('The compendium', 'The completion', or similar), which consists of Middle Kingdom letter formulas and a selection of material from various literary genres. It may have been originally composed during the early 12th Dynasty (c. 2000–1900 BCE), but it was transmitted over several hundred years, and copies have been found all over Egypt, suggesting that it was a core component of the curriculum for scribal students (Kaper, 2010). It was copied well into the Ramesside Period (c. 1300–1000 BCE), despite the irrelevance of the letter formulas by then, but what is curious from the point of view of hieratic palaeography is that it was consistently copied in an archaic style, mostly with a vertical layout in columns separated by dividing lines (Motte, 2022). The style of the hieratic used for this text, in all periods, is modelled on the script as it

Figure 4 A late Ramesside letter (P. BM EA 10375; Wente, 1967: 59–65), written by the village scribe Butehamun to his superior, the general Paiankh. Note the more elaborate writing in the initial lines with the name and titles of the addressee; the pronounced difference compared to the following lines, in more cursive hieratic, is due to the scribe switching between a 'calligraphic' style and a more regular style. Courtesy of the British Museum, shared under a CC BY-NC-SA 4.0 licence.

appears in early Middle Kingdom manuscripts, rather than the contemporary style of the period in which it was copied. This gives copies a very distinctive appearance that allows for the identification of even small fragments as belonging to the text (e.g. Hagen, 2021: pls. 63–65).

It has been suggested that scribes may have felt that an old-fashioned style was more appropriate for literary classics, as opposed to texts composed more recently. Hans-Werner Fischer-Elfert, in a discussion of the hands of Deir el-Medina scribes (c. 1300–1000 BCE), noted that 'The hieratic style of the copies of their own compositions [as opposed to their copies of older classical works] differs in no way from that of the contemporary administrative cursive', citing the case of Amennakht (v) son of Ipuy, (cf. Section 3.5), whose copy of a hymn, perhaps composed by himself, 'has nothing particularly literary about the writing style' (Fischer-Elfert, 2020: 659–660). On this point it might be relevant that when Stephane Polis was researching the hand of the draughtsman Pay (i) from the same village, whose distinct style is found in both literary texts and letters, there was 'no correlation between the quality of the hand and the (literary or non-literary) genre of the text' (2022: 441). It is not straightforward to say how much weight should be afforded to such examples – are they representative or not? – because there is a risk of making a circular argument here: as Polis himself warns (2022: 441), 'It is precisely the fact that his [i.e. Pay (i)'s] hand remains the same across genres that allows us to track this scribe.' As the academic cliché has it, 'more work is needed', and at present it may not be possible to say much more than that each scribe could choose to use a literary register when copying a literary text, or they could choose not to.

3.4 Geographical Variation

The role of geographical variation in the appearance of hieratic is difficult to establish. In most periods there are relatively few sources of data, and when more substantial groups of manuscripts appear, these often cluster in less than a handful of locations. In the New Kingdom, for example, the vast majority of extant manuscripts come from the Theban area, even in the 19th and 20th Dynasties (c. 1300–1000 BCE) when the administrative centre of the state was at the other end of the country. More specifically, some 90 per cent of the ostraca and papyri from this period that have been found in the Theban area come from a single village, Deir el-Medina. This enables relatively fine-grained analysis of hieratic writing at this specific site (Section 3.5) but makes it difficult to generalise on a regional or national level.

There have been attempts to develop criteria for assigning a manuscript broadly to either an Upper or Lower Egyptian origin, but with rather limited success. Möller (1927–36: 2–3) listed eight signs that were allegedly diagnostic, based on the work of Erman (1903: 459–463; but cf. Megally, 1971: xxi). A key case study for Erman was the Great Harris Papyrus (BM EA 9999), which at 42 metres is the longest and best-preserved papyrus in existence. This document purports to list the donations of Ramesses III (c. 1150 BCE) to various Egyptian temples and is divided into five distinct sections, all written in different hands. Sections one through four deal, respectively, with the property of the temple of Amun-Re at Thebes, the temple of Re at Heliopolis, the temple of Ptah at Memphis, and a list of various smaller temples, while section five contains a historical narrative concerning the reign of the king. In the analysis of Erman, the scribes responsible for sections one to three were scribes from these temples, which then represented both Upper (Thebes) and Lower (Memphis and Heliopolis) Egyptian styles of hieratic. While not impossible, this is far from certain. It is true that the sections and sub-sections of the papyrus were originally prepared separately (Grandet, 1994: 32–40), but this merely demonstrates that the process of production was piece-by-piece with a final assembly at the end; there is nothing to suggest that the scribes themselves originated from the temples they wrote about, or that they were trained there. Although the financial data was undoubtedly sent from the respective institutions, the Great Harris Papyrus was probably produced locally in Thebes (Grandet, 1994: 23–26), and the variation in handwriting style – and each style is practically calligraphic compared to contemporary administrative documents – may be as much to do with personal variation as with geographical 'schools' of hieratic (Grandet, 2023: 66). Attempts to apply the criteria of Möller and Erman to other rolls have also yielded ambiguous results, with a single manuscript displaying elements of both supposedly Upper and Lower Egyptian styles (Quack, 1994: 10). The situation up to and including the New Kingdom in c. 1000 BCE is characterised by a low number of sources (except for Thebes), and an insufficient geographical spread: 'It seems doubtful ... that even such a broad distinction [between Upper and Lower Egyptian hieratic] can be established, and there is certainly no hope for differentiating individual hand types of different cities' (Quack, 2017a: 185).

A potentially important case study here is the clay tablets from Balat, mentioned briefly earlier (c. 2500–2200 BCE). Here the variation in hieratic between centre (the governors' palace) and periphery (surrounding villages) leads to a situation where tablets produced at these locations, if they had been 'found outside their archaeological context and in isolation ... would certainly not be ascribed to the same period' (Pantalacci, 2018: 225). The difference here is not simply one of geographical location, however, and social hierarchy probably played a more important role. Scholars have theorised the existence of regional variation in hieratic as far back as the early Middle Kingdom (c. 2000–1600 BCE), but this is often on tenuous grounds, especially when the manuscripts in question do not strictly speaking have a known provenance at all (see Fischer-Elfert, 2021: I, 216, for one attempt).

The situation seems clearer in later periods, although the topic is still relatively understudied; a recent evaluation of the state of research on Roman Period hieratic and demotic (c. 30 BCE–400 CE) analysed local styles at the level of individual institutions like major temples (Quack, 2017a; cf. 2015: 443–444). While this would no doubt be desirable for all periods, the dearth of data, particularly the low number of surviving institutional archives and libraries for the Old, Middle, and New Kingdoms (c. 2500–1000 BCE; Parkinson, 2019; Hagen, 2018, 2019b), makes such an approach difficult. It is not obvious how this situation should be interpreted: would things look fundamentally different for earlier periods if we had more data? Not necessarily. Quack has made the point that in the Roman Period even a geographically small area like the Fayum had 'several seriously divergent writing schools' (2017a: 207), which cannot be demonstrated for earlier periods, and he argued that this late regionalisation of style may be a result of specific historical and technological changes, for example in the training of notaries and the replacement of the brush with the pen. The specific historical circumstances of the Roman Period, when Egyptian scripts were progressively more and more restricted to temples, undoubtedly contributed to the development of local styles of palaeography and orthography at these institutions (Ryholt, 2018: 178). While the topic of different regional forms of hieratic is no doubt worth exploring in more detail for earlier periods too as new evidence comes to light, it seems, on balance, that the ambiguity surrounding the existence of regional variation before the Ptolemaic Period (c. 332–30 BCE) may itself be rather telling.

3.5 Individual Hands

The individual factors that governed the appearance of one person's handwriting in ancient times are not dissimilar to those influencing a modern writer (Morris, 2021). Training and experience are naturally key factors (Figure 5), but so is writing equipment and medium, the speed and concentration of the writer (levels of carelessness and negligence), stress factors, writing conditions (e.g. light and position), and the appearance of the original manuscript which is being copied from. The social context may play a role too, and there is some evidence of family members sharing features across generations, presumably because of the way they were trained (Polis, 2022: 432; cf. Section 5.1).

There was also variation in an individual's style over time, both during the copying of a specific manuscript, where the writing is generally less cursive in the beginning and more so towards the end, and over the years as the individual ages. Perhaps more importantly there was a choice of register: any writer can make a deliberate effort to write in a certain way to improve legibility for others. Not all factors can be analysed in antiquity, but the issue of personal style in writing hieratic is a burgeoning field, and there has been a marked increase in efforts to identify the handwriting of specific scribes in recent years. Earlier scholars often asserted that, for example, the hand on both sides of a papyrus or ostracon was the same, but rarely backed these assertions up with arguments, and the evaluations were largely intuitive, relying on a 'good eye' or gut feeling (Janssen, 2000: 51; Burkard, 2013: 77). Some hands are so distinct, however, that even a non-specialist would not disagree with an impressionistic identification, such

The barber is still shaving, as he reaches evening,
going around with his bag on his shoulder,
as if exiled from neighbourhood to neighbourhood,
looking for someone to shave.
His arms work to fill his ^{belly},
like a BEE which can only eat according to its w0rk.

Figure 5 A limestone ostracon (O. TT 110/2013-140) with *The Instruction of Khety* (Section 7.1–3), written by an inexperienced student. Found in the forecourt of Theban Tomb 110 (Djehuty), probably 18th Dynasty.
The translation is typeset to reflect the disorienting effect of the unpractised hand and the irregular layout of the hieratic on the reader. Image reproduced courtesy of JJ Shirley; photograph by Ayman Damarany, ARCE TT110 Project, 2015.

as the scribe Qenherkhepshef at Deir el-Medina (c. 1250 BCE), memorably described as a veritable *enfant terrible* of hieratic (Sauneron, 1959: xviii n. 7; cf. Figure 6), and a case where both literary and administrative documents are easily recognisable as being in the same hand.

One of the first systematic attempts at identifying hands based on objective criteria was the work of Janssen (1987), who looked at the Late Ramesside Letters, a corpus of documents written by the village scribes Djehutymes and Butehamun (c. 1100–1050 BCE), a father and son. Janssen laid out his methodology, which included looking at the most common words and signs, as these were more likely to be written routinely, and then analysed the different forms of the group 𓊪𓄿 (*p3*) used in both definite

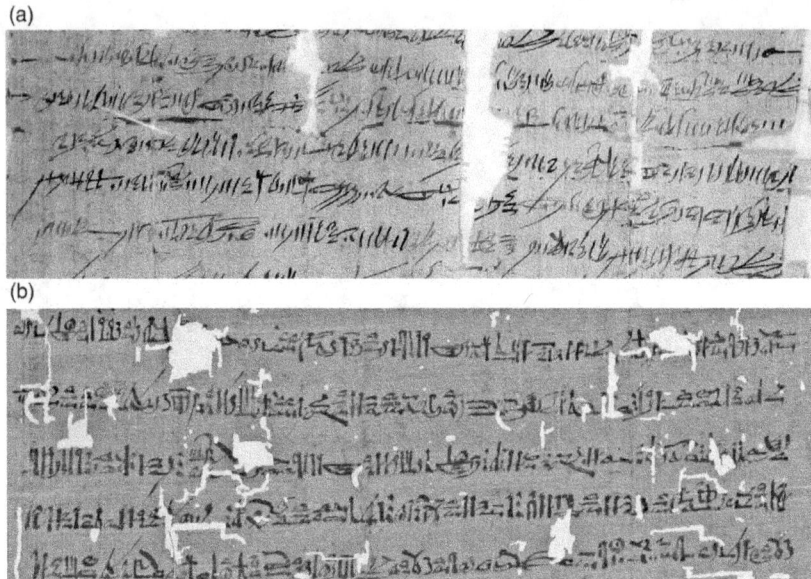

Figure 6 Two images showing the roughly contemporary but very different hands of the scribes Qenherkhepshef (a: P. BM EA 10683, top) and Pentawer (b: P. BM EA 10181, bottom). The papyri, probably written within one or two generations of each other, contain the same composition, *The Kadesh Poem*, but copy 6a is considerably more challenging to read given the cursiveness of Qenherkhepshef's handwriting. Courtesy of the British Museum, shared under a CC BY-NC-SA 4.0 licence.

articles and possessives. His results showed not only that there was some variation in the forms used by a single scribe in a single text, a topic he returned to in another seminal article (Janssen, 2000; cf. Sweeney, 1998), but also that in comparison with a longer administrative document, also by Djehutymes, the more cursive forms were more common towards the end of the document (on both sides), perhaps suggesting a certain fatigue. In the letters of the son, Butehamun, the distribution of cursive versus more elaborate forms tended to differ, at least to an extent, between letters written to his father and those written to his superiors (Janssen, 1987: 165), with more examples of the elaborate forms in the latter. This may have been a deliberate effort to increase legibility or to signal a more formal visual register, as can occasionally also be observed for linguistic registers when subordinates write to their superiors (Polis, 2017a). The variety of forms led Janssen to caution against the use of just a few signs or groups in such an analysis, concluding that 'the range of possibilities within the handwriting of an individual is fairly wide' (Janssen, 2000: 56). His work on Djehutymes and Butehamun has been expanded considerably by others (Demarée, 2018; Miyanishi, 2016), and there is today a consensus that any such analysis has to be relatively holistic, taking into account not just the appearance of individual signs but also groups of signs and words (Van den Berg & Donker Van Heel, 2000), as well as ligatures (Gasse, 2018). The ductus of a scribe is an important part the analysis (Díaz-Iglesias Llanos & Méndez-Rodríguez, 2023: 26–33): this refers to the number of strokes used to form individual signs, the order in which the strokes are made, their layout and segmentation, as well as their direction or orientation (Figure 7), but here too there is room for individual variation within a single manuscript by a single scribe.

An analysis of the Hekanakht letters (c. 1950 BCE), famously used as source material for the setting of Agatha Christie's *Death Comes as the End*, showed that the writer might use anything from two to four strokes for the same sign (Allen, 2002: 193–226). Layout, such as the regularity of the base line, or the size and consistency of line height and line spacing, can also be an aspect of personal style (Gasse, 1992; Dorn & Polis, 2017: 71–72). Similarly, brush-dipping patterns, as well as mistakes and palimpsest traces, have been used as a way to document the writing process of individuals; a scribe might exhibit a tendency to dip his pen at the beginning of sentences, for example, or at the beginning of lines in a manuscript. As Richard Parkinson has noted, this is some of the most direct evidence

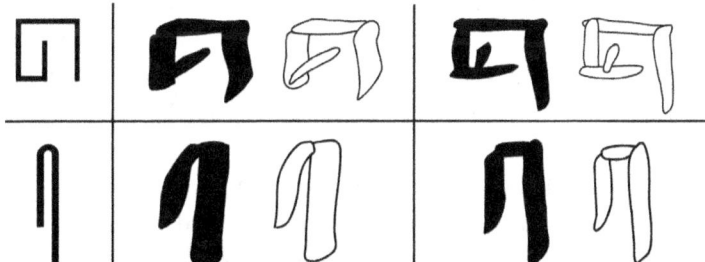

Figure 7 Examples of differences in ductus between two Middle Kingdom scribes. Facsimiles and low-resolution images may obscure this, whereas drawings showing individual strokes in outline clarify the differences. Scribe 2 (right) has added a short horizontal stroke at the bottom of the first sign (⌑) compared to Scribe 1 (left). He has also added a separate short horizontal stroke at the top of the second sign (𐤍), linking the two vertical ones, unlike Scribe 1, whose vertical strokes simply converge at the top. Drawing by F. Hagen, after Allen, 2002; both sets of examples are from letters in the Hekanakhte archive.

we have for the human experience of reading and copying in ancient Egypt (Parkinson, 2009: 90–112; cf. Ragazzoli, 2017b).

The handwriting of New Kingdom scribes from the village of Deir el-Medina (c. 1300–1000 BCE) has been studied intensively the last few decades (Fischer-Elfert, 2020; 2021: 417–425). One of the most promising cases in this regard is Amennakht (v) son of Ipuy, who left behind a considerable range of both literary and administrative texts: praise of cities poems, royal eulogies, hymns, wisdom poetry, and magical texts, as well as work records, legal texts, letters, graffiti, and perhaps even the famous 'gold mine map' (Dorn & Polis, 2019: 18–22; Hassan, 2017). Potentially diagnostic features of his work have been identified (Dorn & Polis, 2017: 67–73; for his linguistic profile, see Polis, 2017b), and this includes not just the shape of the hieratic signs but also aspects of layout, such as kerning between individual signs, number of ligatures, spelling, and ductus (Dorn & Polis, 2022: 443–445; Dorn, 2015: 177–178).

Importantly, this case study can be contextualised to a remarkable degree due to the wealth of material related to the social history of Amennakht. His career history and his work environment, to name just two aspects, are directly relevant to the analysis of his hieratic style: the dated graffiti that he left have been analysed diachronically, and the developments in his handwriting can be observed over time (Dorn, 2015); beyond his regular title as 'scribe of the tomb' for the work in the Valley of the Kings, he also had the title 'scribe of the house of life' – referring to an institution that was a centre for the transmission of religious and scientific texts – which may reflect both exceptional levels of training and privileged access to temple libraries (Dorn & Polis, 2022: 440). However, even when such a comparably rich source of palaeographical data is available, the identification of Amennakht's hand can be difficult because of the methodological challenges outlined earlier (cf. Dorn, 2015: 187–193).

Similar studies have been carried out on material produced by other individuals from Deir el-Medina, such as the scribe of the official journal of the building works on the royal tombs in the Valley of the Kings during the reigns of Ramesses X and XI (McClain, 2018; cf. Morfini, 2019) and the scribe Pay (i) (Polis, 2022), to name just two (see also the list in Fischer-Elfert, 2020: 655).

The co-existence of hieratic and demotic in the Ptolemaic and Roman Periods (c. 332 BCE–300 CE) allows for a comparison of style on an individual level when switching scripts; key examples here are P. Carlsberg 1 & 1a (*Book of Nut*, see Figure 19) and P. Carlsberg 387 & 613 (*Book of Fayum*), where the hieratic text was copied out piecemeal and then translated and commented upon in demotic by individuals who clearly had mastered both scripts (Ryholt, 2018: 182; Beinlich, 2017). One study which compared texts in both scripts being written by a single person detected shared idiosyncrasies in style (Quack, 2017a: 191, 204). The same study also drew attention to the fact that local variations seem more important to the appearance of the script than the genre of the texts being copied (Quack, 2017a: 186; but cf. the caution expressed by Ryholt, 2018: 178–181).

Finally, it is worth bearing in mind that the aesthetic appearance of a hieratic manuscript does not automatically correspond to the care with which a text was copied. As has been remarked for the *Late-Egyptian Miscellanies* (c. 1300–1100 BCE), some of the most conscientious copies with few textual errors are written in the worst hands, calligraphically speaking, and vice versa (Ragazzoli, 2019: 69), and the same has been observed with copies of *Kemit* from the same period (Motte, 2024: 105). Beautiful handwriting, then as now, is not the same as philological competence.

4 Uses

Polis (2020: 558) distinguishes between hieratic 'writing by addition', effectively signs written using ink and a brush, and 'writing by subtraction', where the script is incised. The former is by far the more common, and was used, for example, on papyrus, ostraca, writing boards, ceramic jars and sherds, leather rolls, linen, and wooden labels, and even in some cases on walls (as graffiti in ink – often called *dipinti* in Egyptological literature) or other objects. Incised hieratic was used extensively for graffiti, for example scratched into the cliffs in the Theban mountains, and occasionally also on stelae or on walls, but it seems never to have been conceptualised as a truly monumental script.

4.1 Media

In antiquity hieratic would have been primarily seen as the script of the working scribes and priests, used for writing administrative documents as well as literary and religious texts; the production of documents was not only central to the operation of the state bureaucracy but also seems to have become almost an end in itself (Eyre, 2013). An impression of the vast numbers of papyrus rolls used for accounts, journals, and letters can be gained from looking at surviving institutional archives, even though these are few and fragmentary (Hagen, 2018: 82–115). There can be little doubt that papyrus was the main medium for the use of hieratic, despite the relatively modest number of examples that have survived

(Parkinson & Quirke, 1995). The production of papyrus was a fairly elaborate process of harvesting, cutting up, and arranging fibres of the plant, before drying it, and although not very expensive in absolute terms, the value of a single roll of twenty sheets is estimated to have cost the equivalent of a couple of days' labour (Eyre, 2013: 26–27). Scribes associated with an institution had ready access to papyrus, and there are several examples of extravagant uses of the material in those contexts (Hagen, 2018: 110–111), but the general tendency, especially outside palaces and temples, was to use and re-use a roll for significant periods of time, and to utilise as much of the space available as possible, on both sides. Papyrus is relatively stable in dry conditions, durable, and adaptable: the ink can be easily washed off a page, which can then be re-inscribed after drying; pages can be excerpted and glued together again, and although mechanical wear and tear from repeated opening and closing will strain the fibres, reinforcing strips of papyrus can be glued to the back to strengthen it and make it more durable. Similarly, a roll often had a protective (empty) strip glued on at the exposed end, which would double the thickness to stop it fraying, as well as wrap around to protect it when it was rolled up, much like the covers of a modern book (Černý, 1952: 19). The material flexibility of papyrus meant that it could be folded, expanded, or cut as needed (Krutzsch, 2017, 2019), and so even completely preserved objects come in many shapes and sizes. The length varies enormously, from small Post-it note-sized rectangles with short texts or messages, to almost monumental sizes: the two largest ones preserved today measure a full 37 and 42 metres in length. The height is more standardised, although it changes over time. A full-height roll of the Middle Kingdom (c. 2000–1600 BCE) and the New Kingdom (c. 1500–1000 BCE), for example, is respectively 31–33 cm and 40–42 cm in height, a format which is mainly found in institutional contexts for use when writing administrative documents. Literary rolls were normally half-height rolls (so c. 16 cm or 21 cm in the same periods), or in rare cases also quarter-height rolls (Černý, 1952: 15–17). The front of a roll (the 'recto') is that side on which the uppermost layer of fibres run horizontally, which, perhaps because it was slightly smoother to write on, was normally favoured in the first instance, while the back (the 'verso', where the uppermost fibres run vertically) was used to continue the text from the front, or for other texts. As always, these are tendencies, not rules, and a scribe could choose to write perpendicularly to the roll itself – standard practice when writing letters, for example – which meant that he did not have to think about laying out the text in 'pages' on the sheets of papyrus, but could just write continuously (Figure 8).

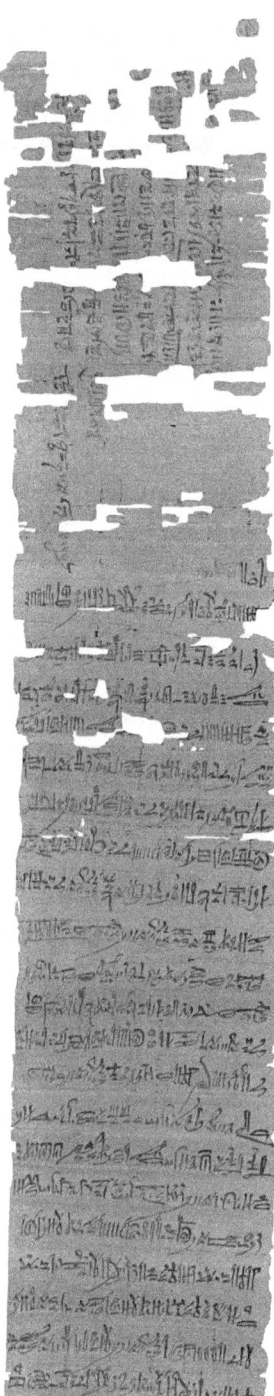

Figure 8 Papyrus Chester Beatty I, a roll with *The Contendings of Horus and Seth* on the front, and a mixture of administrative and literary texts on the back. Shown here is the part of the back that contains a praise poem to king Ramesses V (c. 1250 BCE), where the scribe has turned the roll 90° and written perpendicularly in a fine calligraphic hand. Orienting the roll this way meant that the scribe could write continuously and not worry about the layout of the text. Courtesy of the Chester Beatty Library, Dublin, shared under a CC BY-4-0 licence.

Another medium that was widely used were writing boards, mainly made of wood with a thin layer of white stucco on top, which could be used and re-used almost indefinitely. These were often used for preliminary administrative notes and extracts of literary texts, perhaps for transfer onto papyrus later. They formed part of the basic scribal equipment, often included in two- or three-dimensional representations of working scribes (Figure 9), but were also used in teaching for students to practise their writing skills (Section 5.2).

Many ostraca had a similar function, both in the form of pottery sherds and limestone flakes, although some of these could also have served other uses: extracts of a literary text on several ostraca might be numbered, for example (Posener, 1975), suggesting organisation and storage, and for some exceptionally large ones a didactic use as a form of blackboard has been posited (Parkinson, 2004: 61). Their use in teaching is well attested, even if it can be challenging to identify individual objects used this way (Section 5.2). Administrative ostraca could be written on at different occasions over considerable periods of time (Haring, 2020: 90), but it has often been assumed that most were drafts or preliminary notes to be transferred onto papyrus (Eyre, 2013: 247–248; Donker van Heel & Haring, 2003: 1–82).

(a)

(b)

Figure 9 (a) A wooden model of a granary from the tomb of Gemniemhat at Saqqara (a: ÆIN 1630; early 12th Dynasty, c. 1990 BCE). The scribe is shown seated with a wooden writing board across the knees, with one reed brush in his hand and another behind the ear. The drawing on the right (b) shows the writing board, on which he is recording, in hieratic, amounts of Lower Egyptian barley (*it mḥ*), emmer (*bd.t*), malted barley (*bš3*), and dates (*bnr*; cf. Firth & Gunn, 1926: 272). Photograph by Ole Haupt, reproduced courtesy of the Ny Carlsberg Glyptotek; drawing by F. Hagen.

The extent of the latter is debated, however, with few concrete examples even among the thousands of Deir el-Medina ostraca: whether this is an accident of survival or a real pattern of usage is unclear (Moezel, 2022: 11). Certainly ostraca survive there more numerously in the second half of the 19th Dynasty and the first half of the 20th Dynasty (c. 1200–1100 BCE), as contrasted with papyrus, which we have more of from the second half of the 20th Dynasty (c. 1100–1000 BCE; Haring, 2020: 98–99).

As material objects ostraca are more durable than papyrus and writing boards, which rarely survive outside a funerary context, and they can therefore be used to model the use of writing and the transmission of texts to a much greater extent. Despite their durability their distribution, both geographically and chronologically, is uneven, however, which probably reflects differences in scribal practices over time and in different places. This is likely to be partly a question of pragmatic factors, such as the availability of suitable limestone (abundant at Thebes, less so in other parts of Egypt), but also of local tradition – certainly pottery sherds were available across all sites and in all periods of Egyptian history, even if they were not used everywhere as a medium for writing. Suitable pieces of limestone or pottery could often simply be picked up from the ground, but there are also examples which were worked to a greater or lesser extent, from polished and rectangular pieces that resemble limestone writing boards to roughly shaped pieces where the surface was quickly smoothed (Andreu-Lanoë & Pelegrin, 2018; Pelegrin, Andreu-Lanoë, & Pariselle, 2016).

A category of object that is extremely susceptible to decay, and which is therefore underrepresented in the archaeological record, is the leather roll. Because of the value of the material itself as well as the considerable effort involved in its production, it may have been considered a more high-status medium than papyrus (Weber, 1959: 13–17). There are too few surviving leather rolls to analyse their use statistically, but the extant rolls were used for both literary and administrative texts. They could be constructed from several skins sown together to make a larger roll, and at least one example appears to have been used as a working notebook, similar to papyrus (Figure 10).

In addition to more traditional media such as papyrus, ostraca, writing boards, and leather rolls, others might be used when circumstances dictated. At Balat in the Dakhla oasis, some 350 km into the desert west of Luxor, the distance from the Nile Valley meant that papyrus was less readily accessible (Pantalacci, 2021). In the administration of the local governors, towards the end of the Old Kingdom (c. 2500–2200 BCE), there emerged a tradition of using clay tablets, into which were scratched hieratic signs with a bone stylus (Figure 11).

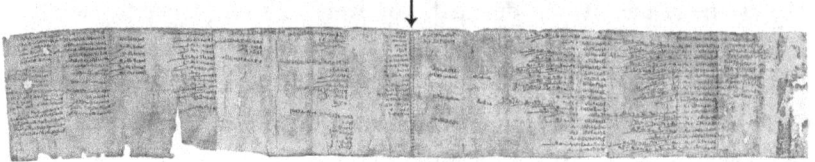

Figure 10 An unusually well-preserved leather roll (185 × 72 cm), used as a notebook by a scribe writing a range of administrative texts in the reign of Ramesses II (c. 1250 BCE). It consists of two pieces which have been sown together with thirty-three stitches: the seam is indicated by the arrow in the middle. The back has two lines with similar content, and at least parts of the front are palimpsest. A section towards the end mentions documents held by five governors, all of which are said to be written on leather rolls, hinting at the discrepancy between ancient use and the surviving archaeological record. After Virey, 1887; text in Kitchen, 1969–1990 II, 789–799, VII, 435–437.

Figure 11 Late Old Kingdom (c. 2500–2200 BCE) clay tablets from Balat, with letters written in hieratic in columns, scratched into the surface with a bone stylus (bottom left). Photograph by Alain Leclerc, © Ifao.

Ink was also used to write on the clay tablets, but the extent of this is difficult to estimate given the state of preservation of the material. In terms of palaeography there are several signs attested only in this corpus, such as a man bowing down with a sickle (determinative of *ꜣsḫ*, 'to harvest'; attested as 𓀢 in hieroglyphic texts), or a potter sitting on the ground and without a wheel, unlike in Nile Valley examples, where he sits on a bench with a wheel in front (cf. Collombert, 2023: 126–127). The restrictions of the medium affected the forms used, in the sense that ligatures were generally avoided: 'keeping the signs separated improved their legibility', because too many deep scratches formed micro-lumps of clay that obscured the signs (Pantalacci, 2018: 219–224).

Hieratic was generally not used for formal inscriptions on monuments, as opposed to informal ones like graffiti, because hieroglyphs were considered the script of choice for display, but there are exceptions. There are some Middle Kingdom (c. 2000–1600 BCE) coffins where texts were written on the sides in ink using the hieratic script, and the signs were then engraved into the wood using a sharp instrument (Willems, 2023), perhaps as a way to ensure it was less vulnerable to accidental or deliberate damage or erasure. In the Libyan Period (c. 1000–700 BCE) there was an increasing number of donation stelae with incised (or 'lapidary') hieratic texts being produced, primarily but not exclusively in the western delta (Jansen-Winkeln, 2017a: 216–217; Fischer-Elfert, 2021: II, 475–489; Lenzo Marchese, 2015), but this may have been due to specific cultural-historical circumstances, and hieratic is otherwise relatively rare in monumental contexts.

It can be worth considering the motives for its use when it does appear, however, as well as the implications. Some small limestone stelae from the Middle Kingdom have short hieratic texts (Fischer-Elfert, 2021: I, 246–250), either incised or written in ink, and especially in the case of the latter this might reflect a limited access to resources. Ramesside examples (c. 1300–1000 BCE) also include private stelae with incised hieratic, which is obviously more labour intensive than a simple ink inscription, but in this period there seems to be a pattern in terms of its use. One such object is that of a sandal-maker (Figure 12).

Here both shape and layout conform to the traditional format of such objects: round-topped with a vignette showing the deceased adoring Horus of Buhen, and five short columns of hieroglyphs above the figures. The rest of the text, however, both below the vignette and behind the figure of Peniunu himself, is written in hieratic, incised into the sandstone. The contents are also unusual: instead of a hymn or prayer, or an autobiographical presentation, the nineteen lines in the cursive script contain copies of legal

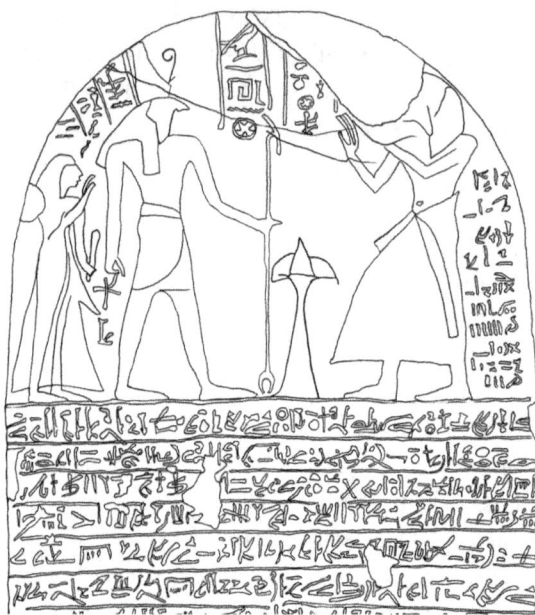

Figure 12 Facsimile drawing of the top half of a sandstone stela (Cairo TR 27.6.24.3, 95 × 48 cm) of the sandal-maker Peniunu. Most of the text is in hieratic, which is very unusual for the Ramesside Period, with only a few hieroglyphs above the figures in the vignette. Drawing by Khaled Hassan and reproduced by his kind permission.

depositions (*r3*) about the use of some land (Hassan & Mekawy Ouda, 2018). Most such Ramesside hieratic stelae were originally displayed in temples (Popko, 2016: 215–217) to an audience of priests and officials who themselves primarily read and wrote hieratic texts. The motive for retaining the original script of the administrative documents being copied from is never made explicit in the sources, but it might be because it lent them authority by signalling that they were copies of original documents written in hieratic, and it would probably have made them accessible to a wider range of readers, too.

A later stela with incised hieratic that is of considerably finer craftmanship than most Ramesside examples is the one inscribed for the famous Amenhotep son of Hapu, a historical character of some importance in Thebes under Amenhotep III, and a figure who came to be worshipped in his own right for much of Egyptian history (Figure 13).

The stela contains a royal decree protecting the personnel of the *ka*-temple of Amenhotep son of Hapu from being recruited by others

Figure 13 Detail of the stela of Amenhotep son of Hapu (BM EA 138), which is a rare monumental use of incised hieratic in a prestigious context. The date in the first line refers to regnal year 31 under King Amenhotep III, but the monument itself was created much later. Courtesy of the British Museum, shared under a CC BY-NC-SA 4.0 licence.

(although it makes an exception for one day a year, for the governor of western Thebes). It presents itself as a copy of an 18th-Dynasty text (c. 1350 BCE), with accurate historical details such as named individuals who occupied important offices at the time, and who are described as witnesses to the royal proclamation. In reality the truth is more complex, because as a physical object the stela and its text are more recent: an analysis of its palaeography, grammar, and orthography suggests a date in the early Third Intermediate Period (c. 1000 BCE), some 350 years later (Möller, 1910). Whether the text is simply a historical 'forgery', or whether it might be based on older documents that were edited and translated into more modern language, is debated (Varille, 1968: 81–85), but the purpose of the text is clearly to give legitimacy to the claims of the temple in its attempts to safeguard its financial interests. The choice of hieratic may be part of this strategy: by casting it in a script that was primarily associated with papyrus, it signals, rightly or wrongly, that it is a copy of a genuine legal document. Things are rarely simple, however, and this specific period is also the one time in Egyptian history when hieratic was used more broadly for donation stelae; it may be part of this wider trend – certainly many of the expressions in the text draw heavily on that genre – but even so, issues of authority and accessibility seem relevant. For a high-status inscription like this, produced in a Theban temple, it was probably not a lack of access to people with the necessary skills that resulted in a hieratic rather than hieroglyphic text.

A less controversial case where one can explore the motivations for choosing hieratic in a context where hieroglyphs would normally be expected is the tomb of Tjay at Thebes (TT 23), from the reign of Merenptah (c. 1210 BCE). On this monument Tjay chose to thematise his professional identity as a 'royal correspondence scribe' (*sẖ3 nsw šʿ.wt*) to an extraordinary degree (Ragazzoli, 2017a: 78–81). Visually this included a famous and unique scene depicting his office in the capital in the Delta, complete with subordinate scribes at work, writing and copying letters to and from the pharaoh (Figure 14).

Tjay's interest in projecting his professional role is also clear in several autobiographical characterisations or epithets on the walls of the tomb (Kitchen, 1969–1990 IV, 109–111). Many statements are more or less formulaic, even if there may have been some historical truth to them ('I was one who attended to the king', 'one praised by his majesty', 'I have spoken no lie'), but it is where he departs from the norm that his personal agenda shines through. He states that he, in his role as royal correspondence scribe, was '[one who repeated] what was said, in order to report the plans/documents (*snn*) to/of every land', that he 'inspected the north and the south for the sovereign' and 'audited this and that'. These statements are in the hieroglyphic inscriptions

Figure 14 A scene showing the 'Place of Letters of Pharaoh' in Piramesse, from Theban Tomb no. 23. The tomb owner Tjay is shown in the middle scene, as well as on the left, here seated in the middle of the room with ten subordinate scribes along its sides, behind a series of columns, sitting on chairs while writing on papyrus. An attendant instructs the porter to 'pour water on the ground … [Make cool] the office! The scribe of correspondence is sitting and writing!' On the right are a series of smaller rooms with chests containing administrative documents – an institutional archive labelled simply 'the place of writings'. After Borchardt, 1907: 59 fig. 1.

around the courtyard of his tomb. In one corner of this courtyard, facing the visitor walking down the central staircase, there is a large inscription incised into the wall in front of a figure of Tjay himself. The material culture is in line with expectations: finely carved signs and traces show it had a painted background in yellow, with red dividing lines between each line of text, but the most striking part of the inscription is the script used. Instead of the hieroglyphs found in the rest of this tomb – indeed in all contemporary tombs – this text is in hieratic (Figure 15).

To a modern visitor this is almost shocking, and it would probably have been no less surprising to the ancient audience. The quality of the incised signs is exquisite, a world away from the contemporary graffiti scratched into the mountains nearby, with a height that makes the script stand out as a truly monumental form of hieratic with signs approximately 3 cm high (Den Doncker, 2023: 239, fig. 139). The text is fragmentary today, but was originally a long and carefully structured biography, where Tjay

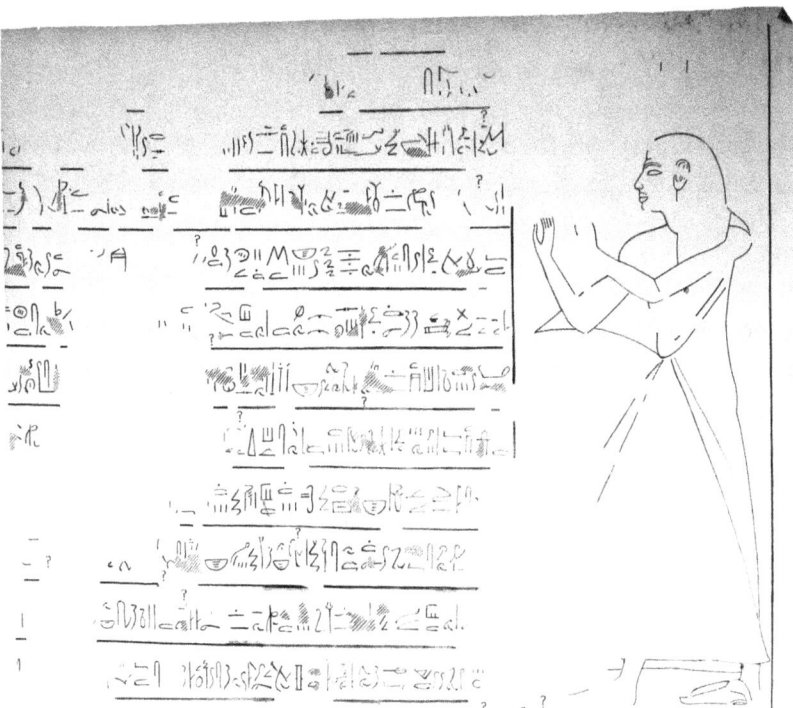

Figure 15 The 'royal correspondence scribe' Tjay stands in front of an autobiographical text written, uniquely, in hieratic. Tracing by Nina and Norman De Garis Davies (Griffith Institute, Oxford, MS Davies 10.10.10). Courtesy of the Griffith Institute, University of Oxford.

expands on his self-presentation, including his scribal duties ('a bag of my letters <to> every land, gathered and sealed').[3] What might the reason be for this unusual choice of script? Like every other tomb owner he knew that most literate visitors to his monument would be far more familiar with the hieratic script than hieroglyphs, but unlike his contemporaries he departed from the expected norm. Seen in context, however, the choice is perhaps not so strange after all: not only was Tjay's daily work in hieratic, but more than most officials he seems to have ascribed his success in life to his professional activities using that script, notably as a letter scribe and diplomat, with a unique set of scenes and statements that projected that part of his identity to his audience.

Beyond the question of motivation and agency, the unusual appearance of the autobiography of Tjay also raises questions about the role of hieratic in the production of autobiographies, and by extension also of other monumental inscriptions traditionally written in hieroglyphs: were such inscriptions first drafted in hieratic? The topic is debated, and there are surprisingly few cases where an initial drafting in hieratic can be demonstrated with certainty (Haring, 2015). One example that showcases the difficulties involved is a Middle Kingdom stela (Figure 16; Cairo CG 20720, c. 1800 BCE; Lange & Schäfer, 1908: 347–348) where most of the text is in hieroglyphs, but where the final lines abound in cursive hieroglyphs as well as many hieratic signs (e.g. 𓀀 as ▰, 𓀁 as ▱, 𓀂 as ◨, 𓀃 as ◧, 𓀄 as ◩, 𓀅 as ◪, 𓀆 as ▤, 𓀇 as ▥, and 𓀈 as the almost ligature-like group ▦).

In this text the hieroglyphs are well formed, suggesting somebody with considerable experience, and the hieratic is confidently executed by a practised hand. The hieratic elements are almost entirely restricted to the last four lines, which might suggest haste or carelessness towards the end of the project, but was the craftsman or scribe also working from a model on papyrus written in hieratic (cf. Fischer-Elfert, 2021: I, 248–250; more examples in Franke, 2013: 52–54, n. 8)?

There are some examples where different 'versions' of a text is preserved both on hieratic papyri and on monuments. One is the wisdom text previously referred to as *The Loyalist Teaching*, a part of which exists both on a private stela from the late Middle Kingdom (c. 1800 BCE) in hieroglyphs and in hieratic manuscripts from the 18th Dynasty onwards

---

[3] The hieratic autobiography of Tjay is still unpublished. E. Frood and F. Hagen are preparing a study of it based on tracings by Nina and Norman De Garis Davies, now kept in the Griffith Institute in Oxford; a preliminary report was presented at the workshop 'Writing in and out of Monumentality: Patterns, Performance, Purpose', at Harris Manchester College, Oxford (5 April 2024).

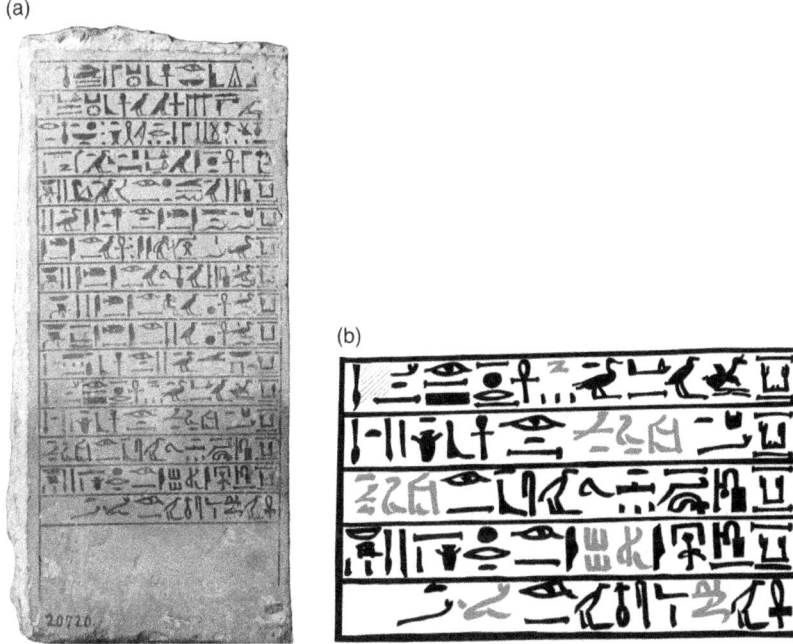

Figure 16 Photograph of a Middle Kingdom stela (Cairo CG 20730) with a list of names and titles painted with ink (16a), and a drawing of the last five lines (16b), where many of the hieroglyphs are replaced by hieratic signs, here highlighted in grey. Image courtesy of the Egyptological Archives, University of Copenhagen, photographed by H. and J. O. Lange; drawing by F. Hagen.

(c. 1500–1000 BCE, Posener, 1976a). The precise redactional relationship between the two versions – is the earlier monumental copy an abbreviated version adapted from an already existing literary text in manuscript form, or is the later text an expanded version of the original monumental copy? – is debated (Stauder, 2020). Whatever the case may be, a comparison between the orthography of the two scripts showed that the hieratic text used more phonetic complements and more determinatives than the hieroglyphic text, which even given the slightly different dates of the sources seems likely to be a consequence of the orthographic tradition associated with the script (Fischer-Elfert, 2021: I, 321–323, cf. II, 600–601). The technicalities of the production process remain unknown, however: could a sculptor convert a hieratic draft into a hieroglyphic inscription in his head, by not only transcribing the individual signs but also by mobilising the different orthographic tradition, all while juggling the demands of layout, orientation, and spacing of signs? Another intriguing example is the relationship between the hieroglyphic inscription on the first Kamose stela and the hieratic version of the same text on the writing board Carnarvon I. These two copies, which are much closer in date than those of *The Loyalist Teaching* just mentioned (both copies are from c. 1500 BCE), have traditionally been directly linked to each other, more specifically with the hieratic version being interpreted as a copy of the hieroglyphic text. Here too the orthography conforms to the respective traditions of the scripts: where the hieroglyphic text abbreviates the word *nḫt* ('strong') to the single sign ⌇, for example, the hieratic text adds phonetic complements and writes ⌇, and in many other words the hieratic text adds determinatives (see Lacau, 1939, with many examples of both phenomena). It is not possible to prove that the writing board was copied directly from the stela, even if most commentators have thought it likely (Enmarch, 2013: 256; Lacau, 1939; Habachi, 1972: 45; Smith & Smith, 1976: 75), and there may have been other hieratic copies in circulation that could have served as a model for Carnarvon I; whether it was this specific scribe – who was described as 'very careless and ignorant' by Gardiner (1916: 107) – or another person who was responsible for the first hieratic copy, the individual in question transferred the text between these two scripts and orthographic traditions. A final example is the depiction and description of the famous Battle of Kadesh where Ramesses II fought against the Hittities (c. 1250 BCE), which can be found on numerous contemporary temple walls and also in a more literary form on papyri (*The Kadesh Poem*; cf. Figure 6), but the manuscripts are clearly not simply copies of the former, so it is difficult to draw any conclusions (Spalinger, 2002: 2–11).

At the same time, it seems plausible that hieratic copies of compositions that were inscribed on monuments existed, even if concrete examples of a papyrus used as a model for an existing inscription may be difficult to find. Such hieratic reference copies were presumably mainly kept in temple libraries and, at least in some cases, in personal collections of papyrus rolls, but they rarely survive. If we had more institutional libraries the situation would probably look different, as the following examples suggest. A hieratic copy of part of *The Book of the Heavenly Cow* from the Ramesside Period (P. Turin Cat. 1982, c. 1200 BCE; Pleyte & Rossi, 1869–1876: pl. 84), for example, was in all likelihood part of a private library of one of the scribes from the village of Deir el-Medina. The same composition is known in monumental form from several of the royal tombs in the Valley of the Kings (Hornung, 1997), decorated by the workmen of the village, but whereas these hieroglyphic inscriptions are always personalised for the king in question, the reference copy on papyrus, in contrast, is explicitly not personalised (using the term *mn*, 'so-and-so', instead of the name of the king; Haring, 2015: 72). Other telling examples are the fragments of the library copies of *The Opening of the Mouth Ritual* from the memorial temple of Thutmose III, also at Thebes (c. 1450 BCE). Here there are several versions of the same composition; one roll written in regular hieratic, perhaps one in cursive hieroglyphs, and, remarkably, an illustrated copy (Hagen, 2024: 191–193). This illustrated copy may have been a model from the building of the temple – the statue depicted is of Hathor, who is known to have had a cult here, but no traces of such a scene has been found in this badly preserved temple – or a copy kept as a reference model for future use, for example for tomb builders. It is interesting in this connection that there is a very similar illustrated version of the same ritual text in the contemporary tomb of Rekhmire (TT 100), but there the accompanying drawings are much more elaborate and the headings are written in hieroglyphs (Davies, 1943: I, 76–77; II, pls. 97–102). The papyrus from the temple is unlikely to have served as a direct model for the scene in this specific tomb, but it demonstrates institutional storage of the kind of document, notably with headings in hieratic, that might have served as a starting point for an artist planning a monumental version of the ritual. One might posit that there was, in some cases, an intermediate stage where a hieratic text would be transcribed into hieroglyphs on a draft papyrus before outlines were drawn on the physical monument, as is well documented with cursive hieroglyphs (occasionally with the odd hieratic sign), but in the absence of surviving examples this remains hypothetical.[4]

Beyond these traditional media and the occasional monumental use, the use of hieratic was very broad. Large building blocks of stone might carry notes in ink stating which work crew was responsible for their production and transport, for example, and the wooden parts of the golden shrines Tutankhamun (c. 1330 BCE) carry instructions on the assembly of

---

[4] The question of whether it is necessary to posit this is also not an easy one to answer. The perceived difficulties of producing a hieroglyphic text on a monument with only a hieratic draft in hand, as outlined by Haring (2015), are not easily dismissed, but the discussion is reminiscent of the one about the existence or otherwise of pattern books in Egyptian art, where scholars such as Laboury (2017) and Den Doncker (2019: I, passim, but esp. pp. 221–223; II, 189–190) have argued persuasively for models where the transfer of motifs by professional specialists does not require such hypothetical pattern books (cf. also El-Shahawy, 2010: 296–297 for an overview of earlier perspectives). The evidence relating to the transformation of drafts of tomb inscriptions in cursive hieroglyphs, quickly written on ostraca in simple black ink, into fully fledged hieroglyphs on the walls of a tomb, suggests that there were artists who carried out this process with considerable skill (Laboury, 2022; Tallet, 2005, 2010). In any case, the hieroglyphic text of the Kamose stela and the hieratic copy on the Carnarvon writing board suggests that a scribe had no problems transcribing a text in that direction, so why not also the other way?

the separate parts in black ink, stating which was meant to face 'north', 'south', and so on, in the tomb (Bell, 1990: 115, with a mix of hieroglyphs and hieratic). At a push, hieratic written with ink could also be used where one would normally use carved hieroglyphs: a set of small model dishes in alabaster, from a foundation deposit near the tomb of Queen Hatshepsut-Meryre (wife of Thutmose III, c. 1450 BCE), has the queen's title and name hastily written on the outside in black ink (Figure 17): despite the softness of the stone there was perhaps no time to customise the objects appropriately with carved hieroglyphs (Hayes, 1959: II, 127–128).

As a cultural practice, the creation of graffiti is attested in most periods of Egyptian history (Peden, 2001; Ragazzoli, Hassan, & Salvador, 2023), and hieratic graffiti can be found across the country, especially in the New Kingdom (c. 1500–1000 BCE). In the Theban mountains the local inhabitants scratched their names into the rock near work sites and paths, as well as in remote locations (Ragab, 2024; Dorn, 2023), and incised graffiti can be found along the trade routes into the desert, or at sites where official

Figure 17 Model alabaster vessels from a foundation deposit in front of KV 42 (MMA 32.2.18-20), with a hieratic inscription reading 'The Great Royal Wife Hatshepsut-Merytre, the Justified'. Courtesy of the Metropolitan Museum of Art, New York, shared under a CC0 licence.

expeditions extracted stone and minerals (Darnell, 2013; Darnell & Darnell, 2002). Examples from sites such as Saqqara and Dashur show literate people visiting the ancient monuments as tourists, leaving their *dipinti* on the stone walls of those buildings that were still standing, as in this case where a teacher and his student or colleague visited the famous step pyramid:

> The scribe Ahmose, son of Iptah, came in order to see the monument of Djoser, and he found it as if heaven itself was in it, Re rising in it. Then he said: 'May bread [and beer], beef and fowl, be provided, along with all things good and pure, for the *ka* of Djoser, the justified. May the sky rain fresh myrrh, and drip incense on it!' By the schoolmaster (*sḥȝ n ꜥ.t-sbȝ*) Sethemheb, and the scribe Ahmose. (translated after Navratilova, 2015: 120)

In this hieratic graffito, the writer manages to demonstrate both an awareness of the past – the monument was over a thousand years old at the time, and there was no tourist information sign telling visitors which king was buried here – as well as his education and training. Wanting to display his literacy may be one part of the motivation behind the act, but he does not merely write his name, instead leaving a longer text whose phraseology is highly formal, and which showcases a command of outdated grammatical forms, as well as knowledge of ritualistic and literary genres. In fact visitors' graffiti become something of a genre itself in this period, with its own rhetoric and formulas, and there are even ostraca showing students being trained in the terminology and formulations (Figure 18; Ragazzoli, 2016; cf. Hassan, 2014).

Contrary to modern expectations, using hieratic to write graffiti in ancient Egypt was not necessarily an ad hoc and informal way of employing the script, but rather an established cultural practice amongst the literate elite, and at least occasionally featured as a part of scribal training. A spectacular and recently discovered expression of this graffiti tradition can be found in a Middle Kingdom tomb at Assiut (c. 1900 BCE), where a great number of people left a broad range of texts on its walls in the 18th Dynasty (c. 1500–1300 BCE). In addition to the common types of simple personal names and visitor's graffiti, there are, unusually, literary classics like wisdom instructions (*The Instruction of a Man for His Son, Hordedef, Kairsu, Amenemhat, Khety*), *The Hymn to the Inundation, The Prophecy of Neferti*, and *Kemit* (Verhoeven, 2020b). The longest is approximately 11 metres in length, following the wall of the chamber, so anyone wanting to read it would have had to literally walk around the room in the writer's footsteps. As a graffiti universe in miniature, it allows for an analysis of practices and priorities in remarkable detail: the tendency to avoid disturbing the original decoration by placing the hieratic text in 'empty'

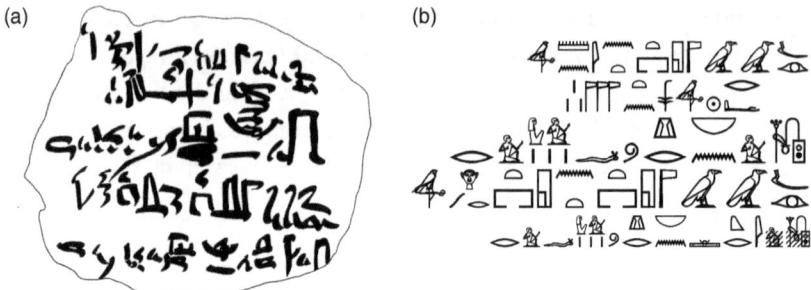

Figure 18 A New Kingdom limestone ostracon (a) (O. UC 31918) with two graffiti formulae (b), stating that the 'excellent scribe' Nebkheruef had come to see the temple of Amun-Re, king of the gods, and the temple of Hathor. The hand – it seems to me to be the work of a single person writing first with more and then with less care and attention – is inexperienced both in appearance and orthography (e.g. inconsistent in the writing of the personal name), and suggests a student being taught the rhetoric associated with visitor's graffiti. Some of the traces have been clarified in the drawing (a) because the ink has almost rubbed off in places. Drawing by F. Hagen.

areas; the dialogue between the graffiti and the older scenes on the walls; clustering of graffiti; and of course the selection of texts themselves, and all that this says about the education and training of the writers (Verhoeven, 2020a, 2023b).

4.2 Genres

Most textual genres are attested in hieratic sources. Administrative documents probably accounted for the vast majority of the texts produced, at least from a purely statistical perspective: records of production or deliveries, accounting tables, daily journals, and letters. Collections of such documents rarely survive in the archaeological record, but when they do, as in the case of institutional archives, they attest to textual production on a vast scale and showcase a range of different types of document (Hagen, 2018). Similarly, individual papyrus rolls that survive because they were removed from their original context, whether institutional or private, and then placed in tombs, give an impression of the level of detail that was recorded. The organisation of workforces was a major concern. There were lists of personnel on building projects; absent workers who were sick, brewing beer, or celebrating festivals; people running away from forced labour; and priests working in temples. Major institutions and projects had bureaucratic structures and procedures in place that generated significant amounts paperwork: a temple or palace would have a daybook with an overview of important events for each individual day (arrival or departure of officials; deliveries and outgoings; copies of letters sent), in addition to individual accounts for activities like baking or weaving (number of loaves per sack; loaves produced by baker; textiles produced per household). A royal dockyard needed to keep track of the timber used for repairs and boat building; a temple would keep track of land owned, flooded, farmed, and ultimately taxed; a fleet of ships collecting grain on behalf of a temple would carefully note down what was received and when; a trading ship would have a logbook with information about goods traded, and with whom; a border fortress would keep records of people crossing the border and their alleged business; and the state managed and reimbursed the builders of the royal tombs, keeping records of their work as well as non-work (in the form of strikes or sanctioned holidays). Legal documents were rarely required but could often be useful to avoid future disputes: sales of objects or properties; adoption agreements; records of accusations, court cases, and witness statements; lists of punishments carried out; and wills and testaments. Communication was another major area of usage, in all periods. Letters were sent to and from institutions and individuals: orders concerning official business or off-the-record assassinations, social updates to family and friends, and even letters to deceased relatives asking them for help and threatening to cut off their offerings if they didn't provide it.

Although numerically rarer in the archaeological record, literary texts were by no means unusual. Again the scarcity of private and institutional collections – libraries – of hieratic manuscripts from most periods probably skews the picture (Hagen, 2019b), but the range of genres attested is considerable. In terms of manuscript history, as opposed to assumed composition dates (Dorn, 2013; Parkinson, 2013), the number of surviving literary texts sees a marked increase in the New Kingdom (c. 1500–1000 BCE). With the exception of the religious texts known as the Pyramid Texts there is very little literary material (in a broad sense) from the Old Kingdom (c. 2600–2100 BCE) overall, and nothing at all in hieratic, although it presumably existed: the survival of long and elaborate religious texts on the pyramid walls of the late Old Kingdom, some of which originated as rituals carried out among the living, probably presupposes a period of transmission on papyrus, but whether this was in hieratic or cursive hieroglyphs is impossible to say (cf. Fischer-Elfert, 2021: I, 173–176). Occasionally scholars have put the composition date for texts only found in later manuscripts in this earlier period, which might imply that they were recorded in hieratic manuscripts, but in the absence of surviving manuscripts it remains hypothetical at best.[5] Even from the Middle Kingdom (c. 2000–1600 BCE) there is only a moderate number of hieratic literary manuscripts but here, particularly due to two or three spectacular finds (the Berlin library, the Ramesseum library, and the Lahun material; Parkinson, 2019), we can see several genres appear for the first time, including literary narratives and poems (*The Story of Sinuhe*, *The Tale of the Eloquent Peasant*, *The Dialogue between a Man and His Ba*, *The Tale of Hay*, *The Tale of the Herdsman*), but also hymns (*Hymns to Senwosret III*, *Hymns to Sobek*), magico-medical literature (spells for a mother and child, protection of individuals and houses, spells against sickness, etc.), mathematical texts, wisdom poems (*Discourse of Sasobek*), and onomastica. Two famous rolls with similar genres such as narratives (*The Story of the Shipwrecked Sailor*) and wisdom poetry (*Ptahhotep*, *Kagemni*) were probably originally found together in a single tomb (von Bomhard, 1999), based on their similar handwriting and state of preservation and clearly reflect a circulation of literary manuscripts among the literate elite.

The same genres are attested and further developed in the New Kingdom (c. 1500–1000 BCE), which in effect represents a high point in terms of the variety of texts written in this script; the period sees the emergence of new genres such as praise of cities, love poetry, illustrated erotic papyri, and divination texts (dream interpretation, oil divination), but also new texts in known genres like wisdom instructions (*Ani*, *Amenemope*, *Amunnakht*), as well as the oldest manuscripts of many texts that may have been composed earlier (*Khakheperreseneb*, which is now attested in the late Second Intermediate Period, *Neferti*, *Hymn to the Nile*, *Instruction of Khety/Satire of Trades*, *Instruction of Amenemhat I*, *Instruction for Merikare*, etc.). One of the important contributions of the New Kingdom evidence is that its richness makes it possible to detect a nationwide scribal tradition which emphasised the same compositions: in effect a national curriculum or literary canon, where knowledge of the classics was itself a form of cultural capital amongst the scribal class. At Deir el-Medina, where the extensive use of pottery sherds and limestone flakes as a medium means that both literary and administrative texts survive in extraordinary numbers, over half

---

[5] The topic is vast and at times controversial. The basic methodological problems, particularly as related to literary texts in a more narrow sense such as narratives, discourses, and teachings, are discussed in Stauder (2013), the articles in Moers et al. (2013), and the detailed review by Jansen-Winkeln (2017b); for a more recent example related to medical texts, see Quack (2022: 93–94), with references.

of the published and unpublished ostraca are literary, broadly speaking (Gasse, 1992: 51), but this is a highly unusual site in terms of literacy, and the transmission of literature here is probably not numerically representative of other places and periods.

Later periods see a gradual reduction in the genres for which hieratic is used; the central role of classical Middle Kingdom wisdom literature in the scribal curriculum declines, for example, with the latest manuscripts from the 26th Dynasty (c. 600–500 BCE; Quack, 2020a). The genre continues to be represented by new compositions, however, like the Brooklyn wisdom text (Jasnow, 1992; c. 600 BCE; for the date see Verhoeven, 2001: 319–326), although most of them are in demotic (*Khasheshonqy*, *P. Insinger*, etc.), not hieratic. There might be a similar trend in other genres because there are relatively few scientific manuscripts with magical, medical, and astronomical texts from between the seventh and fourth centuries BCE (Fischer-Elfert, 2021: II, 525–537), but issues such as publication bias and uneven survival patterns perhaps distort the picture (Lieven and Quack, 2018; Quack, 2023b). As outlined earlier (Section 2), the emergence of demotic and the fact that hieratic became mainly a temple script had fundamental implications for the types of text copied and composed in hieratic, eventually leading to a situation where the vast majority of hieratic texts were religious in nature.

4.3 Hieratic Used to Write Non-Egyptian Languages

As a script, hieratic could also be used to write other languages than Egyptian (Quack, 2010a). New Kingdom (c. 1500–1000 BCE) examples include the London Medical Papyrus (BM EA 10059; Leitz, 1999: 49–50), which contains, alongside traditional Egyptian recipes and treatments, a series of incantations written in hieratic but in languages that are clearly not Egyptian. These are specifically against skin diseases considered to be foreign and are labelled as non-Egyptian ('in the language of foreigners'), but with both headings and ritual instructions in Egyptian ('… to be spoken four times …'). They appear to be mainly in an early form of North-Western Semitic (Leitz, 1999: 61–63), while another incantation is described as being 'in the language of the Cretans' (Lange, 2007: 49). Other examples include an ostracon found in the Valley of the Kings which has an Egyptian text on one side and what is possibly an administrative note in Phoenician concerning goats on the other (Cairo JdE 25759; Shisha-Halevy, 1978); an incantation for lion-hunting in the Harris Magical Papyrus, which has been identified as Semitic (Leitz, 1999: 49–50); a short sentence in *The Satirical Letter of Hori* also in Semitic (P. Anastasi I 23.5; Fischer-Elfert, 1986: 198–199); an undeciphered text perhaps in a Nubian language (P. BM EA 75025 verso; Demarée, 2006: 26–27); and finally a papyrus with spells against snakes in what seems to be proto-Berber ('in the language of the Qeheq'; P. Turin 54030, see Silvestri, 2023). These examples are part of a broader cultural process of interaction which finds its expression also in a significant number of Semitic loanwords in Egyptian texts (Hoch, 1994), as well foreign names rendered phonetically using hieratic (Schneider, 2023), but longer passages of foreign languages in hieratic are still relatively rare, and a notable proportion of those that have survived are incorporated into magico-medical texts.

As the script of the Egyptian administration, hieratic was also used in areas under Egyptian influence outside the country itself. Hieratic texts, including literary ones, have been found at Amara West in the Sudan, for example, but these are clearly the product of Egyptian scribes living and working there in the Egyptian administration (c. 1500–1300 BCE; Parkinson & Spencer, 2017). To the north of Egypt, in the Levantine area, a number of administrative ostraca have been found that also show hieratic being used, perhaps both by Egyptian and Egyptian-trained scribes. More interestingly in the latter case is that local scribes who wrote texts there in Hebrew used hieratic for writing numerals and certain measures of volume (of grain). This practice was a direct legacy of the Egyptian administrative presence, and notably persisted for several hundred years after the Egyptian state no longer held direct power in the area (c. 800–500 BCE; Wimmer, 2008: 272–281; 2018).

4.4 Layout, Paratextual Marks, and 'Space Fillers'

In the earliest periods, hieratic was largely written in columns, read from top to bottom, but at some point in the late Middle Kingdom (c. 1800 BCE), scribes started to write in horizontal lines instead, from right to left. The reason for this change is never stated in the ancient sources, but may have to do with both speed and an efficient use of space, in the sense that more signs can be fitted on a page when writing in lines. The development was gradual and intermittent, with some literary manuscripts displaying writing in both columns and lines in a single text written by a single scribe (e.g. P. Berlin 3022 with *Sinuhe*, P. Leningrad 1115 with *The Shipwrecked Sailor*, and 1116B with *The Prophecy of Neferti*; Parkinson, 2009: 93). In subsequent periods most texts were exclusively written horizontally from right to left, often in 'pages' with a line length of 20–25 cm – this corresponds to a natural limit for the human eye's ability to follow a text without resorting to tracing the line with a finger – but beyond this basic principle hieratic texts could be laid out on the page in a number of ways.

The simplest method was to use the contents themselves as a structuring device, with one line per entry (or name) in a list, for example, or even one clause per line in a literary text, although the latter was in practice rare (Winand, 1998: 164–168). Red ink was often used to mark the start of sections and paragraphs (Posener, 1951b), but even so it was not a trivial matter to find the relevant section of a long text. In a medical roll like the Papyrus Ebers, which at 20 metres long and with 110 columns of text is the best preserved of its kind, the scribe added numbers above each column to facilitate orientation among the numerous treatments and recipes. Numbering pages in a papyrus roll, or even sequential copies of a text on ostraca, does not seem to have been a common practice, at least not in earlier periods (Posener, 1975), but there are quite a few examples from the fourth century BCE onwards. Not surprisingly this is attested mainly in copies of rather long texts, and these notably include a range of different genres, including literary narratives, ritual texts, and other religious compositions, where it may be less about improving accessibility and more about carefully prepared copies (Ryholt, 2018: 168–172).

Some documents were ruled, ranging from Old Kingdom tables of accounts (c. 2500 BCE) with individual cells with both horizontal and vertical dividing lines, to a simpler format with only horizontal lines running across the length of the page between every two to three lines of text (Parkinson & Quirke, 1995: 38–39). Later periods saw a development with a more varied and frequent use of ruled lines to lay out a text: some Roman Period rolls from the Tebtunis temple library (c. 100 BCE–200 CE) display formats where every line of text is ruled, or where each page is clearly demarcated by double ruled lines at the top, bottom and the sides, framing the text. At least in this temple this practice is much more common with hieratic manuscripts (c. two thirds) than with demotic ones (c. one in eight), perhaps because the former are more likely to be carefully prepared cultic manuscripts (Ryholt, 2018: 162). Such use of lines could be quite creative, and one example with *The Book of Nut* (P. Carlsberg 1; Lieven, 2007) shows a tabular structure where lines beginning at the first margin line (i.e. to the extreme right) contains the beginning of each hieratic section, which is then translated and commented upon in demotic, giving a convenient way for the scribe to orient himself in the document when looking for commentary on a specific line of the original hieratic text (Figure 19).

Using orderly straight lines to lay out a text before it was written was not the only option available. When space was limited, on both ostraca and papyri, the layout of a text might be cramped, and scribes occasionally inserted lines after the copying to separate columns; these were ad

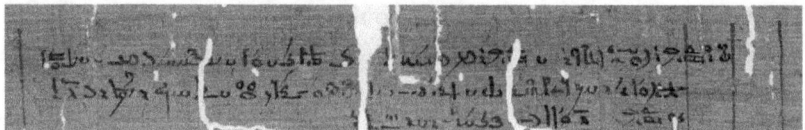

| Occurring | of the redness after birth. 'The redness occurs after birth': (This means) when he rises with the colour that the sundisk has in the morning, namely Re, so that his rays on earth are in said colour. Look at the picture. The 𓇳 is that which should be read as 'the redness'. |

Figure 19 The layout of *The Book of Nut* in P. Carlsberg 1, using vertical lines to structure the text. Top: the original manuscript (col. 2, lines 1–3). Bottom: a modern translation with the same layout (mirrored). Italics signals words written in hieratic, while the following translation and commentary is in demotic. Courtesy of the Papyrus Carlsberg Collection, Copenhagen.

hoc and followed the margins of the text (Figure 20; cf. Winand, 2020b: 18 figs. 5–6, 32 fig. 29).

Hieratic was very much a working script, and like all such scripts it displays traces of scribal practice that are detectable to a much more limited extent in a monumental script like hieroglyphs; paratextual marks and signs that show scribes annotating, organising, checking copies, erasing and editing (Polis, 2020: 556–557; Verhoeven, 2020a: 95). In an administrative document this might for example take the form of checkmarks in lists of names, a practice which highlights the processual aspect of the writing act: such documents are not simply copied and archived, but drawn up, read, and annotated according to real-world circumstances, like the presence or absence of workers (Winand, 1998: 35). Similarly, accounting documents might have a hieratic sign like ⌃ in the margin next to a line, meaning that the commodity listed had been 'delivered', or an ostracon might have the sign ⚏ written in large strokes across several lines of text, signalling that it had been 'copied' into a larger journal on papyrus (Jüngling, 2021).

Corrections in hieratic manuscripts were sometimes carried out by simply erasing the words and then writing the correct ones in their place, but they could also be made by inserting the missing words between the lines or columns, or by inserting a red cross above the line to indicate missing text, which would be complemented by another cross in the margin or at the bottom of the page along with the missing signs (Motte & Sojic, 2020: 74–75). Words or entire entries could be struck out in red or black ink and then replaced by additions above the line (Winand, 1998; Ragazzoli, 2019: 67–68), or be singled out by circles or brackets to indicate that they should not be read (Verhoeven, 2020a: 99–102; for a Ramesside example, see Motte, 2024: 104). If an omission was too substantial for an

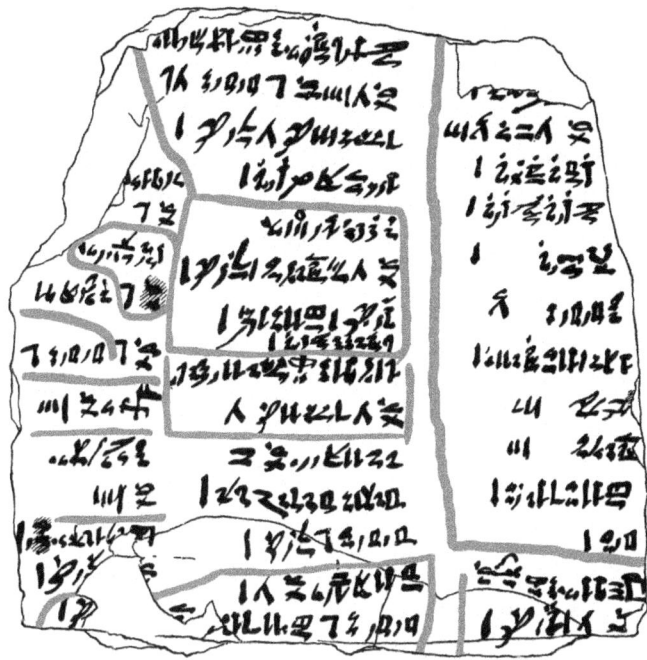

Figure 20 A limestone ostracon from Deir el-Medina (O. Petrie 31 = O. UC 39639), with lists of bread, beer, cakes, fish, and various types of oil given to some men and women, written in three columns. The dividing lines were added after the text was inscribed in order to demarcate the individual lists. Adapted from Gardiner and Černý, 1957: pl. 35 n. 1.

intra-linear insertion, it could, depending on the type of text, be inserted a considerable distance from its rightful place, as in a case from *The Book of the Dead* of Nu (BM EA 10477) where the paratextual mark ⋏ in red ink signals the placement of the omitted section a full ten columns of text later in the manuscript (Verhoeven, 2020a: 108). Precisely when corrections were undertaken can be difficult to say with certainty; in the latter example, it must have been some time after the mistake was made since it involved the continued copying of ten columns, but in other cases it may have been done almost instantly. The identity of the person making the correction is often debated, but where it is possible to tell, self-correction rather than by a teacher seems more plausible (Hagen, 2012: 97–98).

Hieratic at its most basic is a continuous script devoid of typographical indicators of textual division, but although scribes never used modern markers such as space between words, commas and full stops, there were other tools available. A relatively common feature of hieratic manuscripts, mainly found in copies of literary texts and model letters, is the presence of red dots ('versepoints') above the line that, in a broad sense, mark syntactical units (Ragazzoli, 2019: 65–67; Tacke, 2001; Winand, 1998: 169–175). These punctuation marks, which are attested primarily in the New Kingdom (c. 1500–1000 BCE), were an integral part of the hieratic training of a scribe, and they could be employed in surprising contexts: some cuneiform tablets from Amarna display the characteristic Egyptian versepoints superimposed, in red ink, above the incised cuneiform signs in the clay (Izre'el, 1997: 46–47, pls. xix–xxx). In these literary texts the presence of versepoints demonstrate that they were read (and annotated) by Egyptian scribes locally, perhaps as part of their training in the Akkadian language, complementing the evidence from Akkadian–Egyptian dictionaries found at the same site (Hagen, 2019b: 246–249; Izre'el, 2001: 481–490). Many copies of *Kemit*, with its characteristic layout in columns and its archaic hieratic style (Section 3.3), have short horizontal dividing lines within the columns that also clearly reflect a conscious effort by the scribe to mark divisions between syntactical units, and so are functionally comparable to the versepoints found in texts written horizontally. Typographical markers like versepoints and dividing lines are never consistently used for specific genres and or compositions, and even *Kemit*, which is quite conservatively transmitted in terms of layout and style of hieratic, only has dividing lines in about 35 per cent of the copies (Motte, 2024: 95).

In the same way that rubrics were used to mark the beginning of a section, the end of a section could also be marked by inserting the sign ⸺, probably as an abbreviation of the word 𓎼𓂋𓎛 (*grḥ*) meaning 'completed, finished'; this is especially common in religious texts such as the Coffin Texts (Enmarch, 2020: 48–50), magical and medical texts (Motte & Sojic, 2020: 68–69), and in copies of the *Late-Egyptian Miscellanies* (Ragazzoli, 2019: 64–65). The end of a whole text, at least for religious and literary compositions, would normally be marked by the insertion of a colophon, ranging from a simple 'it is finished' (*iw=f pw*), to a more elaborate version that might include the titles and names of the copyist, a dedication to his superior(s) or teacher(s), and a statement that it had been copied accurately (Luiselli, 2003). A famous example, from a *Book of the Dead* of the 18th Dynasty (Cairo CG 51189, c. 1400 BCE; Munro, 1994: pl. 71) written in cursive hieroglyphs, states that 'It is finished, from beginning to end, according to how it was found in writing, copied (*spḫr.tỉ*), verified (*sḥsf. tỉ*), collated (*smtr.tỉ*) and checked sign for sign (*smḫ3 tỉ.t r tỉ.t*)' (Lenzo Marchese, 2004). Colophons were used after the final section of a composition even when that particular physical copy was only an extract of a larger whole, which demonstrates an awareness of the status of the extract as the end of a larger composition. Individual sections or chapters of a text were called a 'house' (*ḥw.t*) in Egyptian, and could be numbered 'first chapter', 'second chapter', and so on, as seen on a possibly 26th-Dynasty copy of *The Instruction of Amenemope* (P. BM EA 10474, perhaps c. 600 BCE; cf. Verhoeven, 2001: 301). Many extracts from literary texts on ostraca correspond to such chapters, and one text from Deir el-Medina suggests that students there may have been asked to copy one chapter per day (Fischer-Elfert, 2021: II, 377–379).

5 Scribal Training in Hieratic

Egyptian scribes, who were at all times a tiny minority of the population (Baines & Eyre, 2007), were primarily trained in the script which they would be using on a daily basis, which from the third millennium until the sixth century BCE would have been hieratic (Fischer-Elfert, 2021: I, 11). Precisely how this training was organised and carried out is often difficult to reconstruct, at least in the earlier periods; the strikingly homogenous nature of the script (both orthographically and palaeographically) might suggest a degree of coordination on a national level (Quack, 2017a: 207–208), but to what extent most scribes were trained in schools or as part of apprenticeships is debated (Lazaridis, 2010). There is some evidence for the training process itself in the form of texts copied by beginners, exercises in writing grammatical paradigms, and so on, but mainly from the New Kingdom onwards (c. 1500–1000 BCE; Motte, 2022; Venturini, 2007). This evidence can be informative about both the methods of instruction and the contents of the curriculum (Section 5.2).

As the role of hieratic changed over time, so did its relation to scribal training. When abnormal hieratic and demotic gradually replaced hieratic as the everyday script of choice, a process that took place around 700–500 BCE, the use of hieratic was in effect reduced to priestly communities. For them, the ability to read and copy the large number of older religious texts written in hieratic necessitated the preservation of knowledge of this style of writing, and those wishing to become priests might be examined in hieratic. A key document from Tebtunis, dated to 162 CE, records in Greek how two candidates for the priesthood were examined to see if they were of priestly families and so could be admitted as priests. One was able to demonstrate his eligibility because of his parentage, while the other provided 'proof of a knowledge of hieratic and Egyptian writing (by reading) from a hieratic book produced by the sacred scribes' (P. Tebt. 291; Messerer, 2017: 181–191, no. 40; Grenfell,

Hunt, & Goodspeed, 1907: 58). In this later period, such knowledge was in practice restricted to priestly families, and so served as evidence of a suitable background, but how was knowledge of hieratic acquired in earlier periods?

5.1 Schools, Apprenticeships, and Training

In order to be able to read and write, scribes and priests were evidently taught, but details about the setting for this remain remarkably elusive for most of Egyptian history. There are some references to schools in literary texts, perhaps most famously in *The Instruction of Khety* (also known as *The Satire of Trades*), where a father is taking his son to the capital ('The Residence') in order to attend 'school' (lit. 'room of instruction in writing', ꜥ.t sbꜣ.t n.t sẖꜣ; Jäger, 2004: 131), along with other children of high-ranking officials. The implication is probably instruction in hieratic rather than hieroglyphs, as the text continues with a reference to scribes occupying 'any office of the Residence'. The text stresses the value of attending the institution ('A day at school is beneficial for you') and provides some contextual information suggesting that teaching took place in the morning (Jäger, 2004: 131, 149, 153). Along similar lines, but in much more detail, a *Late-Egyptian Miscellanies* manuscript includes an often quoted passage in which the writer describes sending somebody to school:

> I have placed you at the school (ꜥ.t sbꜣ), together with the children of officials, in order to teach you and to instruct you regarding this office which can improve (your lot). Look, I am explaining to you the nature of a scribe in his (daily duties). Quickly to your place! The writing is (already) in front of your friends, so get your clothes and careful with your sandals. You should bring your papyrus roll daily with consistency, and you should not be idle. They say: 'Three plus three'. You check other (texts) sign by sign, until the box [is full?]; another happy occasion in which you have understood a papyrus book! Do more, in producing 15 further 'mats', and ... for a lifetime, then finish by reading a letter. You will learn to do calculations silently; do not allow (your) voice to be heard, [nor any sound] from your mouth. Write with your hand, read with your mouth, and take advice (from those who know more than you). Do not be lazy, do not spend a day being idle; this is bad for your body! Adapt to the nature of your teacher, and listen to his instructions. Act like a scribe: 'Here I am', you should say as often as [he calls] to you. Beware of protesting (?). (translated after P. Anastasi IV, 22.3-7; cf. Caminos, 1954: 262–263).

Like *The Instruction of Khety*, this extract links access to school with people from a privileged background, the 'children of officials' (*ms.w sr.w*; Ragazzoli, 2019: 279, 414–415), and despite some minor difficulties of translation, the passage paints a vivid picture of schooling in practice: bringing writing materials along daily, the pupil is advised to be diligent, attentive, and respectful to his teacher, and the skills taught include mathematics and silent calculation, careful checking of documents ('sign by sign'), reading aloud, and letter-writing, all implicitly related to hieratic texts. Another mention of school in a literary text is in *The Blinding of Truth by Falsehood*, where the son of Truth was 'sent to school (*ʿ.t-n-sbȝ*, lit. "room of instruction")*, where he became exceptionally skilled at writing, and he practised all forms of fighting, surpassing his older friends who were at school with him', and where he was bullied for not knowing the name of his father (Simpson, 2003: 105; Gardiner, 1932: 32.10–13). *The Instruction of Any* also has a short reference to the addressee having been 'placed in school (*ʿ.t sbȝ*)' by his mother, where he was 'taught to write' (Brunner, 1957: 19), but with no further details.

Other less explicitly literary sources include an unusually detailed biographical sketch on the statue of a Ramesside priest called Bakenkhons (c. 1250 BCE), who mentions in passing that he 'was a man of Thebes from my father and my mother, the son of the second priest of Amun in Karnak. I came out from the room of writing (*is n sḫȝ*) in the temple of the lady of the sky as an excellent youngster' (Frood, 2007: 43), which is normally taken to mean that there was a school at the temple of Mut. Another priest in the same period, Anhurmose, states that he 'was a humble youth who sat upright in the school room (*ʿ.t sbȝ.t*)' (Frood, 2007: 109), and he presents this institution as a setting in which he excelled by displaying cleverness, intelligence, and an ability to learn.

A likely setting for this would be temples, where the children of priests could receive instruction that would prepare them to take over their father's offices. Much of the evidence is circumstantial, like the discovery of a number of literary ostraca in a part of the memorial temple of Ramesses II, which has been interpreted as evidence of a school-like institution there (Barbotin & Leblanc, 2023; Barbotin, 2013, 2023; Leblanc, 2004; but cf. Hagen, 2012: 78–79), or the ostraca from other temples nearby that show beginners' handwriting (Section 5.2). Precisely what this would look like is difficult to establish, and nothing like the fourth-century CE school at Amheida (Cribiore, 2015) has been found in earlier periods, nor need one have existed. The latter was an explicitly Greek type of institution, and there is no indication that a physical room specifically designed for instruction existed in Egyptian temples. The evidence from the seventh century BCE to the second century CE is, with the exception of the earlier material from Deir el-Medina, arguably the best documentation we have for educational practices in ancient Egypt, even if it is less relevant here as most of this training involved demotic, not hieratic (overview by Prada, 2018).

In theory at least, teaching in temples was under the authority of an 'Overseer of teaching' who belonged to the priesthood (Quack, 2002). Each of the four groups (*phyle*) of priests in the temple had such a teacher, and he is explicitly said to be responsible for teaching the children of priests, to decide who is qualified for a temple career. This information comes from a normative text (*tp-rd*) written in Middle Egyptian known as *The Book of the Temple*, a manual describing how Egyptian temples should be organised, which survives in approximately fifty copies. Almost all of these date from the first and second century CE – one possible copy, in hieratic, may be from the 26th Dynasty (c. 650–550 BCE) – but its date of composition was certainly earlier, perhaps even as early as the late Middle Kingdom (c. 1800 BCE; Quack, 2016b: 104–107), so it was certainly in circulation in periods when hieratic was the main script in use. In terms of curriculum this source is instructive, even though it cannot be taken as a generalisation; scribes in the state bureaucracy were in all probability trained with a different set of priorities. For priests, *The Book of the Temple* lays out a process consisting of an initial examination of those selected for a temple career, followed by four distinct levels or modules (*sp*) of further education. The initial evaluation or entry exam consists of the teacher 'reading the writings of the children of the prophets (*ḥm-nṯr*), the lector-priests (*ḥry-ḥb*), and the high-ranking priests (*wᶜb ᶜꜣ*)', and these 'writings' most likely refer to texts in hieratic. The first module of the advanced training is then described as introducing them to 'God's words' – that is, hieroglyphs – as well as the 'customs of Upper and Lower Egypt', religious geography, and perhaps the etiquette of the royal palace (alternatively, royal purification and protection spells; Ryholt, 2005: 161). The second module seemingly refers to memorisation, the preservation of the festival scroll, and 'solving the problems of all writings', that is, the study of texts in depth. The third is all about medical texts, while the fourth deals with divination (eclipse *omina*) and texts relating to embalming. The content of this education was clearly related to the specific skills and knowledge needed by priests, and shows, amongst other things, that hieroglyphs were taught secondarily to basic reading and writing in hieratic (Quack, 2021).

References to schools are relatively rare, however – the sources presented earlier account for no small part of what is available for the pharaonic period – and there is little evidence for a formal and widespread system of schooling, despite systematic searches for it (e.g. Brunner, 1957). This rarity is particularly surprising given the tendency of Egyptian scribes to thematise their own identity, experience, and the ideology of literacy: it has even been described as 'the great absence in the [*Late Egyptian*] *Miscellanies*' (Ragazzoli, 2019: 133) and raises the question of whether another model for training may not have been more widespread, specifically in the form of apprenticeships.

The most extensive and detailed evidence of teaching hieratic dates to the New Kingdom (c. 1500–1000 BCE), and in the second half of that period specifically from the village of Deir el-Medina at Thebes. It is worth looking at this in some detail as a secular and non-royal context for the transmission of writing skills, despite its unusual character as a highly specialised community. There was probably no school building as such here, but groups of children may have been taught together (cf. Gasse, 2000 for a potential teaching area), and there is a passage in the Late Ramesside Letters where the scribe Djehutymes writes to his son Butehamun to 'not let the young boys who are in school (ꜥ.t sbꜣ.t) cease studying' (Wente, 1990: 180). This may relate to an early stage of training, characterised by basic copying exercises in order to practise the mechanical skills of writing (Section 5.2), as well as an initial introduction to the various genres relevant for a future scribe, from model letters to classical literature. The 'school' referred to may be less a physical location than a social institution. It is noteworthy, however, that the Egyptian term for 'school' here (ꜥ.t (n) sbꜣ.t, 'room of instruction') survives as a term for over a millennium, and even exists in Coptic as ⲁⲛⲥⲏⲃⲉ (Černý, 1976: 9), which might suggest that it had a more central cultural significance as a concept than one might otherwise think based on the modest number of attestations in contemporary texts. At the same time – although this is perhaps related to a more advanced stage of learning – there is evidence that training in the form of individual apprenticeships was common in the village, with younger men working under or beside their fathers or other family members. Several colophons mention 'assistants' (ẖry-ꜥ) dedicating their work to their 'masters' or 'teachers' (nb), for example (McDowell, 2000), and where the details of social relationships between those being trained and those training them can be studied, there is ample evidence of colleagues teaching each other's sons (Baines & Eyre, 2007: 92–94; Bickel & Mathieu, 1993). In this context it is worth noting that the study of the hand of Pay (i) from Deir el-Medina by Polis (2022) included a methodologically important section where he also looked at the hands of his son and grandson.

The conclusion was that there was a 'filiation of hands', where several features – including orthographic peculiarities such as writing the preposition hn^c as 🗝 – were shared by the three generations of draughtsmen, resulting in a broadly similar appearance. There were enough differences to distinguish them from each other, however, including patterns of pen-dipping, the consistency (or otherwise) of the straightness of lines, spatial layout of signs, and the forms of certain common groups (including *p3*).

The richness of the Deir el-Medina material notwithstanding, this model of apprenticeship training is unlikely to have been a New Kingdom (1500–1000 BCE) phenomenon, and already in the Balat clay tablets from the late Old Kingdom (c. 2500–2200 BCE) there are examples with very poor handwriting, suggesting trainee scribes; importantly, these have a precise archaeological context, and were found stored with other more fluently written texts (Pantalacci, 2018: 226), perhaps suggesting junior apprentices working alongside more senior scribes.

In later periods of Egyptian history training in hieratic became limited to the education of priests, and this is reflected in the hieratic material from, for example, the temple library of Tebtunis (c. 200 BCE– 200 CE; Ryholt, 2020a; Quack, 2006). Large numbers of cultic and funerary compositions were transmitted as hieratic copies, and these could be updated with a translation and commentary in demotic to make sure that their content remained accessible (for *The Book of Nut*, cf. Figure 19). The process of training in these later periods is also evident from material produced by or for students.

5.2 Evidence for the Training Process

In the absence of a clearly defined schooling system (Section 5.1) the learning process must be largely reconstructed based on the products left by the scribal activities, and this process itself will have been heterogenous and varied, depending on the social context, the priorities and methods of the teacher, and the skill and learning ability of the student. Generalisation is difficult, and the following is merely a selection of some illustrative sources, not an exhaustive list of stages and methods (for a systematic presentation and categorisation of ostraca from a teaching context, see Gasse, 2005).

The two media that have traditionally been associated with scribal training are writing boards and ostraca, but mainly those carrying literary texts (Venturini, 2007: 14–27). This is not a very nuanced approach, and several of the criteria that have been advanced for the identification of specific copies as exercises can be problematic when analysed in detail (Hagen, 2012: 93–99), but a significant proportion were probably produced during scribal training. The initial stages, when students simply copied an individual sign again and again, are not very well represented in the surviving material (Venturini, 2007: II, 19–50), but there are some illustrative examples, such as an ostracon with a grid system into which a student has copied the hieratic signs for 𓂑 and 𓂝 repeatedly in two columns (Figure 21; CGT 57300; López, 1980: pl. 95).

There is more evidence for intermediate and advanced stages of training, with a range of different types of exercises, mainly on ostraca. The most common are those where forms are practised by repeating certain groups of signs and numbers, as well as onomastic or lexical exercises, and exercises in writing royal or private names (Venturini, 2007: I, 46, 52–99; on model letters, see now Quack, 2023c). Grammatical paradigms are exceedingly rare but probably relate to training in some sense; one has a series of conjugations with the element *iw* followed by various suffix pronouns (*iw=i, iw=f, iw=n, iw=w, iw=sn, iw=t*), while two others focus on the verb *ḏd*, 'to speak', and a conjugation table (Venturini, 2007: II, 206–211). Despite their rarity, paradigms have been found in several locations (including Thebes and Abydos), which may suggest similar teaching methods across the country (Fischer-Elfert, 2021: II, 357–358).

Figure 21 A photograph of a Ramesside limestone ostracon or writing board (a) showing a student practising some individual hieratic signs (𓂝 and 𓂑) inside a grid system, with a drawing of the same object (b) that shows the faded ink more clearly. The other side, not shown here, is not as well preserved but shows a similar layout with other signs. Courtesy of the Egyptian Museum, Turin, shared under a CC-0-1.0 licence.

The exercises provide evidence of some level of abstract linguistic consciousness (Uljas, 2013: 4), but it is not easy to link this to a specific stage of teaching because it is difficult to evaluate the quality of the hands in such short texts.

Because of its rather peculiar style of hieratic (Section 3.3), *Kemit* was widely used in the training of scribes, as evident in the more than 500 extant copies, and as a group these manuscripts often reveal interesting details about the didactic process. This includes cases where an initial copy in red ink was written over in black ink by somebody tracing the strokes (Motte, 2024: 93–94; Gasse, 2005: 107). An 18th-Dynasty (c. 1500–1300 BCE) writing board from Thebes has a set of columns from *Kemit* written by a confident and fluent hand, followed by the same passages in an untrained hand: evidently this represents a teacher who wrote out part of the text and then asked his pupil or apprentice to copy it sign by sign (Galán, 2007). A similar situation can be found on another writing board from the same period, where a teacher has written out the opening lines of *The Hymn to the Nile* on one side, and a student has copied the same lines on the other side (Hagen, 2013). The same method is visible on some ostraca, on which a teacher has copied a line for the student to repeat several times underneath (Figure 22).

In this example it is not only the hand and the uneven distribution of signs that reveals the inexperience of the student, because even in this short line there are several places where he has misunderstood the teacher's

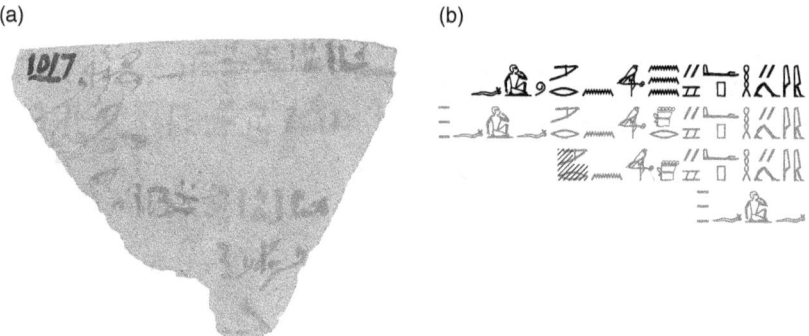

Figure 22 A Ramesside limestone ostracon (a) (O. DeM 1195; Posener, 1951a: pl. 40), with a line by a teacher at the top ('The Nile Flood comes to the one whom he loves'), followed by the same words repeated twice in an inexperienced hand underneath. A modern transcription into hieroglyphs (b), using a computer program, does not communicate the inexperience and irregularity of the student hand. Photograph by Alain Leclerc, © Ifao.

writing: he has added an additional vertical stroke after the water group which yields the group 𒀭 rather than the intended 𓏤𓈗, and then had to add another vertical stroke to represent the divine determinative; he has misinterpreted the verbal ending 𓈖 as the suffix pronoun 𓆑; and he has added plural strokes (𓏦) at the end, although they are not present in the original (Venturini, 2007: II, 133). These mistakes are repeated almost identically in the last line. Here is a student who had been told to copy a line written by his teacher, but whose ability to understand what he was copying was limited. He was not an absolute beginner, however, and his misreading demonstrates his familiarity with signs not present in the model text.

A group of *Kemit* ostraca shows a series of red dots after each word or phrase (i.e. not traditional versepoints that mark clauses; Section 4.4), which has been interpreted as evidence of post-copying checking, whether by a copyist/student or a teacher (Motte, 2024: 101). The poor handwriting of some manuscripts that include *Kemit* was initially interpreted as a sign that it was among the very first texts to be copied during scribal training, but this view has been modified slightly in recent years (Gasse, 2005: 90). It has been pointed out that the unfamiliar direction of writing and the deliberately archaising style might account for the unevenness, and that even more experienced students could have found it challenging (Mathieu, 2003: 121). Its use in scribal training is not generally disputed, but the majority of copies are in experienced hands and fluently written, which may suggest that it belonged to a more advanced stage of training (Motte, 2024: 100).

Texts copied by teachers for students can be suggested in a few cases, but rarely proved unless they also feature student hands, as in the cases set out earlier. Some exceptionally large ostraca have sometimes been thought to represent blackboards, but the size of the signs on these objects is not that different from a regular ostracon, and would have necessitated students sitting very close to them when copying the text (Parkinson, 2009: 200 n. 48).[6] There are also jars with hieratic literary texts from Deir el-Medina that have unusually large signs (c. 1.6–2.0 cm tall, with some up to 3 cm) which might also be an indication that they were meant to be used in a teaching context (Venturini, 2007: I, 34; Gasse, 1992: 57), and there are some unprovenanced and unpublished papyrus fragments with

---

[6] The most famous examples are the two ostraca with *The Story of Sinuhe*, the first in the Ashmolean Museum (dimensions: 88 × 31.5 cm) and the second in Cairo (22 × 106 cm), but there are others which approach them in size, including one at the French Institute in Cairo: O. DeM 1204 + Berlin P. 14934 (originally at least 30 × 80 cm, but probably larger) with *The Hymn to the Nile*, *The Instruction of Amenemhat I*, and *The Instruction of Khety* (Posener, 1951a: 26, pls. 43–43a; Jurjens, 2024: pls. 10–13).

exceptionally large signs too, which may have come from a similar social context.⁷

The examples discussed earlier are all from the New Kingdom (c. 1500–1000 BCE), and although hieratic ostraca from later periods are rare, some have been found in different temple contexts, and these are probably also to be linked to priestly training. Among the almost 1,500 or so ostraca from the 'House of the Ostraca' in the temple at Narmouthis (Kom Medinet Madi, c. 150–300 CE), kept and partly organised as teaching materials, there is a handful in the hieratic script (Caputo, 2019: 97–99; Vandorpe & Verreth, 2012). This includes one piece that shows a student writing individual words in hieratic, and then rendering them in the Old Coptic alphabetic script. The example shown in Figure 23 has words for different deities and epithets (?), including Ḥḏ-ḥtp.t, 'Hedjhotep' (god of weaving), bnw.t, 'The Baboon' (?), mtr, 'The Accurate One', ʿḥʿ, 'The Standing One', and 'Imn, 'Amun'.

The text appears to be the product of a priestly student learning to read hieratic, in effect an exercise in vocabulary: the hand seems inexperienced because of the awkward layout of the signs, resulting in some determinatives having to be put on the next line. The mixing of scripts in the Narmouthis material, seen also in the glossing of hieratic and demotic texts with Greek letters, illustrates the emergence of Old Coptic (Quack, 2017b; Blasco Torres, 2015). A comparable but much larger recent find of ostraca from the temple of Athribis (c. 300 BCE–200 CE) includes a number of hieratic ones that, once published, will undoubtedly shed much light on the teaching of the script there; according to Ivan Guermeur, this find has effectively doubled the number of known hieratic ostraca from the Greco-Roman Period (Boud'hors et al., 2021: 101–112). One revealing example has some lines from the Daily Temple Ritual written in an unpractised hand with notes in a more experienced demotic hand below, naming a certain 'Besa son of Pausir the young, who recites the hymns', perhaps implying that this is a copy made by a student priest who had to learn hieratic in order to fulfil his duties in the temple. As this ostracon hints at, some scribes and priests in later periods of Egyptian history were trained not just in the hieratic script but also in the grammar and vocabulary of earlier

---

⁷ The papyri in question are P. Carlsberg 127 and P. Brooklyn 37.1786E, which have hieratic signs that are respectively c. 4 and c. 6–7 cm tall. The date and provenance are uncertain: the former is perhaps Ptolemaic (c. 300–100 BCE?), based on the palaeography, and was bought from Maurice Nahman (for which see Hagen & Ryholt, 2016: 253–256). The latter came to the Brooklyn Museum from a nineteenth-century collection, via the New York Historical Society, and is therefore not from the famous Wilbour group from Elephantine. Only a few signs are visible in its current state of preservation, so its date is unknown. On other late papyri with over-sized signs, see Quack, 2020c: 23.

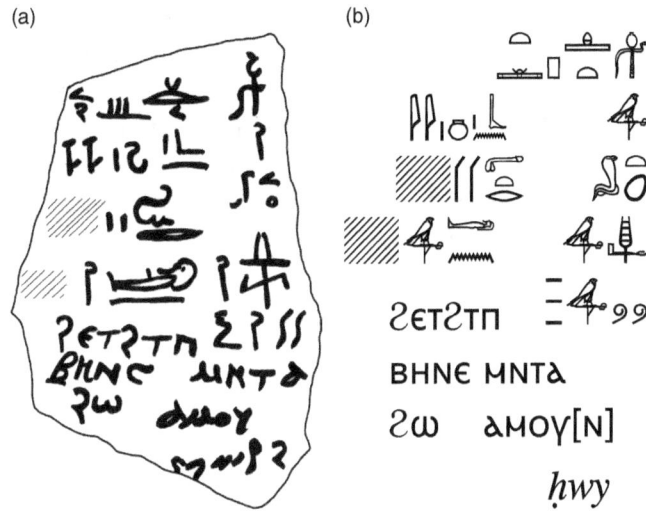

Figure 23 An ostracon from the temple of Kom Medinet Madi (O. Narmouthis 35) with a student exercise, perhaps from the second century CE, in facsimile (a) and with a transcription (b). At the top are words in hieratic in a slightly awkward hand, with the phonetic values written out in Old Coptic underneath (the last line is in demotic). Drawing by F. Hagen (based on Gallo, 1997: 4–5, pl. I, including corrections by Quack, 1999a: 195).

stages of the language. Naturally this went hand in hand with advanced training in hieratic, and there are examples of 'translations' between different stages of Egyptian, such as a papyrus where passages in Middle Egyptian were rendered using early demotic wording and grammatical structure, but where both were written using the hieratic script (Quack, 1999b). At such advanced stages of training, it can be difficult to distinguish between a student and a teacher, or even decide if a text represents training at all. A Roman Period (c. 50–150 CE?) hieratic writing board with a list of verbs of motion, for example, or a roughly contemporary papyrus with a long word-list (onomasticon) structured into various categories, could be the work of either, or none – a highly educated expert, effectively researching the ancient history of his own language, might leave very similar texts behind (Fischer-Elfert, 2021: II, 582–589).

5.3 Relationship to Other Scripts

Hieratic is derived from the hieroglyphic script and started out as a simplified version of it, adapted for rapid writing with a brush and ink (Haring, 2023). Broadly speaking this means that any one hieratic sign corresponds to one hieroglyphic sign, but over time the scripts diverged, with hieratic developing a tradition of combining sign groups written in such a way that the individual signs are not always clearly visible (the combinations are called 'ligatures' in palaeographical studies). Both scripts remained inherently visual in nature, and shared what Stéphane Polis has called a 'figurative potential', whereby new signs, clearly depicting real objects, might be introduced where necessary: for hieratic this can include signs that are not present in the contemporary hieroglyphic script (Polis, 2020: 554–555; but cf. Verhoeven, 2023a: 2). As writing systems hieratic and hieroglyphs are very similar, even if there are minor differences: where hieroglyphs can be written both left to right and right to left, hieratic is almost invariably written from right to left. The orthography of hieratic texts also tends to be slightly different from hieroglyphic ones, often displaying a more restricted set of determinatives and a tendency to provide more phonetic complements, probably to aid legibility (Quack, 2010b: 238). Statistically there are more hieroglyphic signs than hieratic ones (Verhoeven, 2023a: 2), but absolute numbers are not necessarily very revealing about usage, as both groups include a number of unusual signs. How many hieratic signs a scribe used in daily tasks, or had to know in order to read common types of texts, is not known, but perhaps it would be possible to make some estimates (on hieroglyphs, see Quack, 2010b: 243–244, as well as his comments on demotic on the subsequent pages).

Hieratic co-existed in all periods with other scripts, and the mutual influence of these on each other is well documented. In earlier periods when most literate people were primarily trained in hieratic there are numerous cases where a text, whether written in ink or incised in stone, includes hieratic forms mixed with other scripts such as hieroglyphs or cursive hieroglyphs (Graefe, 2015; Lenzo Marchese, 2015). Occasionally such mixing may have been deliberate, but more often it seems to be an accidental feature, influenced by the scribe's extensive training in and daily use of hieratic, as opposed to his more limited experience with the monumental script. In periods where proficiency in hieroglyphs was rarer, as in the First and Second Intermediate Periods (c. 2100–2000 and 1600–1500 BCE), when the absence of the centralising power of kingship meant a decline in associated workshops and specialists, there was an increased influence of cursive forms in hieroglyphic inscriptions (Haring, 2015: 75–76). In later periods, the mixing of demotic and hieratic groups in a single document is not unusual (Fischer-Elfert, 2021: II, 523–525), and here too there are both accidental and deliberate examples: a good example of the latter is the demotic P. Rylands IX, where as part of a long presentation of a person's claims to a priestly office, the text of two stelae are cited as evidence in the case, and the text of these two objects are included, but written in hieratic (Fischer-Elfert, 2021: II, 538–540). Hieratic in turn also influenced the hieroglyphic system. An early example is the hieroglyph ℯ (*w*), which is based on the hieratic sign ʃ, used as an alternative to the quail chick 𓆑, and in Ptolemaic temple inscriptions (c. 332–30 BCE) the new hieroglyphs 𓊗 and 𓊘 are derived, respectively, from the hieratic groups 𓎛 and 𓎟, for which the corresponding hieroglyphs were originally 𓊝 and 𓊞 (Kurth, 1999: 94–96; for New Kingdom examples, see Meeks, 2007: 7–10).

Between hieratic and the more artistic hieroglyphic script, there was a style known as 'cursive' or 'linear' hieroglyphs which was used primarily for religious texts: it is common on coffins and tomb walls, and can occasionally also be found on papyrus and ostraca (Díaz-Iglesias Llanos, 2023). In the context of portable media it is perhaps best known as the script associated with *The Book of the Dead* (Lucarelli, 2020), but this may be a distortion caused by patterns of survival: funerary texts are statistically over-represented in our data because they tend to survive better than non-funerary manuscripts, and the contexts in which many of the latter would have been kept – temple and palace libraries, for example – rarely survive. In terms of its place in the scribal culture of ancient Egypt, and more specifically its relationship to hieratic (Allam, 2007), it is probably significant that it appears quite regularly in the few collections of literary material that survive, above all in rolls with ritual texts (Hagen, 2024: 193–194; Parkinson, 2019: 118–119). Advanced training in the script is perhaps visible in a Deir el-Medina ostracon where the literary classic *The Instruction of Amenemhat*, which is normally written with horizontal lines of hieratic, has been copied in columns using cursive hieroglyphs instead (Figure 24).

Conversely, a text normally written in cursive hieroglyphs, like *The Book of the Dead*, was occasionally copied in hieratic instead (Verhoeven, 2023c: 170–175; Lenzo Marchese, 2023: 88–90), and the same is true of the archaic script used for *Kemit* (Motte, 2024). In appearance cursive hieroglyphs represent a compromise between the extreme iconicity of hieroglyphs and the economy of a cursive script (Konrad, 2023), but without sacrificing the former, so that a reader trained in hieroglyphs can read cursive hieroglyphs without much difficulty. Its relationship to hieratic is perhaps less straightforward, although these two scripts are in practice often mixed. In the funerary texts in the tomb of Nakhtmin at Thebes (TT 87, c. 1450 BCE),

Figure 24 Two limestone ostraca (top: LACMA M80.203.204; bottom: BM EA 6523, right) that carry the same text, *The Instruction of Amenemhat I*, come from the same village, date to the same period, but are written in, respectively, cursive hieroglyphs and hieratic. Top: Courtesy of Los Angeles County Museum of Art, public domain image. Bottom: Courtesy of the British Museum, shared under a CC BY-NC-SA 4.0 licence.

for example, painted on the walls in cursive hieroglyphs, there are several examples of hieratic forms of individual signs; these show a concentration in areas where working was difficult (in corners and on the ceiling), where the attention of the copyist might be challenged by both physical and psychological factors, but many others were distributed 'randomly and in a practically spontaneous manner' (Díaz-Iglesias Llanos, 2022: 146; Lüscher, 2015).

Most periods provide examples of such script mixing, including in the Greco-Roman Period (c. 300 BCE–400 CE), where hieratic texts on papyrus might be provided with demotic glosses, or vice versa (Quack, 2015: 457; cf. Figure 19). Certain texts might mix the scripts according to specific criteria, as in an astrological text where 'sacred' words would use the older script and more prosaic ones would be written in demotic (Fischer-Elfert, 2021: II, 594–595; Dieleman, 2005: 52). Supralinear annotations – perhaps known as *sẖ-bl*, 'outside-writing' in Egyptian – in a different script than the main text often relate to issues of legibility and accessibility; these can shed important light on linguistic training and knowledge (Dieleman, 2005: 48–62). A telling example is a set of second century CE papyri from the temple library of Tebtunis, which contains, in exquisitely drawn hieroglyphs, copies of inscriptions from monuments which by then were over 2,000 years old: the tombs of the nomarchs of Assiut (Osing & Rosati, 1998: 55–100, pls. 6–12). The hieroglyphic texts on the papyri were reproduced in a manner that matched the ancient layout on the tomb walls (largely in columns), and their purpose seems to have been pedagogical, used in the training of priests in older linguistic stages and scripts. To that end they contain numerous glosses in the younger scripts demotic and Old Coptic, but also signs and words in hieratic, suggesting that proficiency in hieroglyphs marked an even higher level of specialisation. Rather surprisingly, the use of these specific tomb inscriptions to teach hieroglyphs finds a parallel in modern Egyptology, where students have been reading them as part of their own training for several generations, since at least seventy years before the Tebtunis papyri were identified (Sethe, 1924: no. 30). In other words, ancient students read the exact same texts some 2,000 years earlier. The glosses in these papyrus rolls are essentially reading aids; some are repetitions of rare phrases in the hieroglyphic text, repeated in hieratic next to them or in the margin below (functioning almost like the notation '*sic*'), while others help with syntactical understanding. Figure 25 shows one example where someone, probably a senior priest, has added some hieratic signs before and after a title reading 'confidante of the king' (*mḥ-ib nsw*).

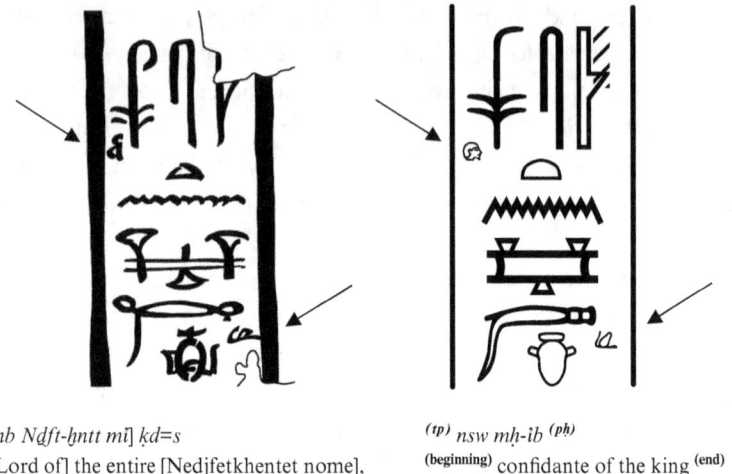

[nb Nḏft-ḫntt mi] ḳd=s
[Lord of] the entire [Nedjfetkhentet nome],

(tp) nsw mḥ-ib (ph)
(beginning) confidante of the king (end)

Figure 25 Facsimile drawing (left) and transcription (right) of a detail from P. Carlsberg 305; the manuscript is from the temple library of Tebtunis and is dated to the Roman Period. It contains a copy of the hieroglyphic inscriptions of the tomb of Khety II at Assiut, built some 2000 years earlier. The tiny signs in hieratic next to the dividing lines are meant as reading aids for those studying the text. Drawing by F. Hagen.

The writing of the title in the hieroglyphic text inverts the grammatical sequence of the signs (giving the literal reading 'king, confidante of'; the sign ⇌ seems to be a mistake), in line with the Egyptian principle of 'honorific transposition' whereby names and words for gods and kings are written first in a phrase regardless of where they should be positioned grammatically. Honorific transposition is a familiar problem to modern students of Egyptian, and it clearly posed a challenge for students in the ancient temple too, so in order to help the reader, the two tiny hieratic signs ᛃ (⊛) and ⌒ (ᛚ), which read 'beginning' and 'end' respectively, bracket the difficult title and signal that the hieroglyphs belong to a single phrase (Osing & Rosati, 1998: I, 77; II, pl. 7). The social context of these papyri – Roman Period priests learning hieroglyphs with the help of notes written in hieratic – is comparable to that of the famous Tanis Sign Papyrus (BM EA 10672; Griffith & Petrie, 1889; Quack, 2023a; cf. Quack 2020d), a carbonised manuscript of which only fragments remain. The text contains columns of large drawings of individual hieroglyphs, with a thin pen and with plenty of details, followed by columns listing the corresponding sign in hieratic with a regular brush, and then finally the Egyptian name(s) of the hieroglyphs in hieratic (Figure 26).

Hieratic 67

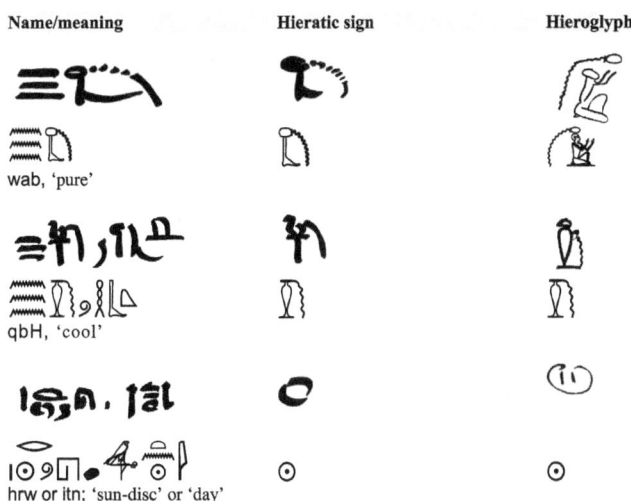

Figure 26 Three entries from the Tanis Sign Papyrus (BM EA 10672) with transcription and translation. The entries are not sequential in the original manuscript, and the hieratic signs have been partly restored to enhance legibility. Drawing by F. Hagen.

The scribe who drew up the tables was aware of the divergent traditions of hieratic and hieroglyphs, and how different signs were used: in the first example, the hieroglyphic sign 𓐍 is not simply repeated in hieratic, but rather substituted with the sign that would normally be used to write 'pure' in a hieratic text, namely 𓐍. Again the implication is that scribes were expected to know hieratic before they advanced to hieroglyphs.

An interesting case where hieratic occurs alongside a non-Egyptian script are the cuneiform tablets from the 'Foreign Office' archives at Amarna (c. 1400 BCE). Here Egyptian scribes received letters from rulers in the Levant, and on some of the clay tablets they wrote annotations in ink with details about when the letters arrived, who brought them to Egypt, and where pharaoh was at the time, or they simply noted that the letters had been 'copied' or 'circulated' (Figure 27; Hagen, 2011; 2016: 165–166).

Hieratic could also be used to 'translate' texts from different Egyptian scripts and writing systems; an intriguing example is an ostracon in Turin (O. Turin CGT 57440, c. 1250 BCE) that on one side has columns of so-called enigmatic or cryptographic writing using cursive hieroglyphs, while the other has a transcription into hieratic. The object seems to be the result of a 'decoding exercise' where the cryptographic composition, a funerary text in honour of Amennakht (v) son of Ipuy (perhaps a copy of a now lost

Figure 27 A letter on a clay tablet (EA 23 = BM E29793), written by the ruler of Mitanni to Pharaoh Amenhotep III (c. 1350 BCE), concerning the sending of a statue of a goddess to Egypt. Upon the arrival of the letter in the Egyptian capital, a scribe added a note in hieratic in black ink underneath the cuneiform text, with the date of receipt and the location of the pharaoh at the time. Courtesy of the British Museum, shared under a CC BY-NC-SA 4.0 licence.

inscription in his tomb), was copied, interpreted, and parsed into syntactical units, and then finally 'translated' into hieratic (Polis & Seyr, 2023).

In the New Kingdom (c. 1500–1000 BCE), especially at Thebes, there was another graphic communication system in use that is known to Egyptologists as identity marks (Haring, 2018). This system of signs was non-linguistic in the sense that it consisted of symbols representing individuals that could be inscribed on objects like jars or tools in order to signal ownership. Functionally this has been called a 'pseudo-script': because it was composed of symbols for individuals, it could also be used in administrative contexts, and there are examples of attendance lists of workmen where identity marks are used instead of their names written in hieratic, as was the standard practice. The persons responsible for these 'texts' were in some cases almost illiterate, while in others they display at least a limited knowledge of hieratic too. One example is a duty roster from the reign of Ramesses III (c. 1150 BCE), which has a date, in hieratic, in the top right corner, a series of daily entries, ⸗ for *sw*, 'day', followed by hieratic numbers, and then identity marks, signs for commodities, and finally amounts (Hagen, 2011: 77, 119). It is rare to find such a regnal year date in hieratic in connection with a list of identity marks (Haring & Soliman, 2014: 78–80), but it demonstrates the way in which the different script systems could be integrated, and implies that at least some individuals were familiar with both (Haring, 2018: 179–180, 234–236).

6 Modern Research Tools

There are many tools available to those interested in hieratic, and the following section provides a short introduction to more general literature, the main palaeographical works, and some online resources. Specialist publications for the topics discussed elsewhere in this Element can be found in the reference list.

6.1 Handbooks and Overviews

Hieratic studies have recently seen the publication of several important introductions and overviews. The most detailed is H.-W. Fischer-Elfert's magisterial *Grundzüge einer Geschichte des Hieratischen* (2021), which presents the main corpora of material in chronological order, with a number of interesting comments about the individual texts, as well as a host of methodological insights distributed throughout. This two-volume work is complemented by a volume of teaching aids for hieratic of the Old and Middle Kingdoms (Möschen, 2021; a forthcoming one by M. Landrino on the New Kingdom has also been announced), which contains pedagogical tips, exercises, and a handy sign-list based on the appearance of the hieratic signs. The latter can be useful for students trying to identify a specific sign by its shape, because the main palaeographies are instead organised around the thematic groups of the corresponding hieroglyphs. Shorter overviews of hieratic, many of which are worth consulting as they complement each other, include Verhoeven (2023a); Grandet (2023); Polis (2020); Gasse (2016); Wente (2001); and Posener (1972); references to older contributions can be found in these.

6.2 Palaeographies

After the groundbreaking work of Champollion in the first decades of the nineteenth century (Section 1), the main contribution to the field of hieratic studies in terms of palaeography was the work of Adolf Erman on Papyrus Westcar (Erman, 1890: II, 32–60, tables I–VII), in which he included a systematic comparison with manuscripts from the 12th to the 22nd Dynasties (c. 2000–700 BCE) as a way of dating that papyrus. Although this was an early attempt using a limited amount of material, the resulting date of late Second Intermediate Period (c. 1650 BCE) is accepted even today. Erman's methodological influence on his student Georg Möller is evident in the latter's three-volume *Hieratische Paläographie. Die Ägyptische Buchschrift in ihrer Entwicklung von der fünften Dynastie bis zur Römischen Kaiserzeit* (Fischer-Elfert, 2021: I, 49–50). First published between 1909 and 1912 (second edition, 1927–36), Möller's work used material spanning most of Egyptian history, and was a monumental achievement for the time, as evidenced by the fact that it has remained the key resource for both students and scholars working with hieratic texts for over a century. It is only in the last few years that the digital database AKU-Pal (Section 6.3; https://aku-pal.uni-mainz.de/) has slowly begun to replace it. He also published three companion volumes with examples of texts for teaching (Möller, 1927–35), which again has remained the standard work until the present, although it is now partially superseded for the Old and Middle Kingdom by Möschen (2021). Möller's *Palaeographie* has some limitations which are well known to specialists, such as a focus on mainly literary manuscripts and a selective list of forms – a volume on administrative texts was planned but never published before his untimely death – and some of his conclusions regarding the development of the script need to be adjusted (Sections 3.1 and 3.4; cf. Verhoeven, 2019: 1171–1172), but overall his meticulous approach resulted in a remarkable reference work. A slight source of frustration for many students is that the ordering of signs in his palaeographical tables follows a thematic grouping according to the underlying hieroglyphic signs, rather than any similarity of form or sequence of strokes, so that it is no easy job to find the often handful of hieratic signs that most resemble each other (Fischer-Elfert, 2021: II, 439–441). Möller's initial efforts have since been supplemented with palaeographies of certain periods or types of texts, and there are now chronological studies of the earliest hieratic (Regulski, 2010), of the Old Kingdom (Goedicke, 1988), of administrative ostraca of the New Kingdom (Wimmer, 1995), and of literary hieratic of the first millennium BCE (Verhoeven, 2001), to name just a few, and many text editions include extensive discussions of palaeography as it relates to a single manuscript or groups of manuscripts; this is now gradually being collected and incorporated into the AKU-Pal database.

6.3 Online Databases

The most important online resource for hieratic studies is undoubtedly the AKU-Pal project (https://aku-pal.uni-mainz.de/), which not only aims to eventually replace the old palaeographies of Möller and others but also to make available metadata (media, dates, provenance, etc.) of both old and new sources (Gülden, 2016); since going live in 2022 it has been continuously updated. A useful resource for both teaching and research is the New Kingdom Hieratic Palaeographies (http://nkhp.uliege.be/) website, which combines data from various hard-copy palaeographies as well as from AKU-Pal, and where one can search and compare shapes according to genre of text by entering transliteration, Gardiner hieroglyphic sign codes, or entries from Möller, and even produce exercises for memorising signs. *Trismegistos* (www.trismegistos.org/) is a key resource whose broad diachronic remit marks it as one of the first ports of call for scholars looking for information on specific hieratic manuscripts, including texts from later periods of Egyptian history. Two other databases of note, if a bit older, are those dealing specifically with hieratic material from Deir el-Medina: Deir el-Medine Online is a Munich-based database of non-literary ostraca with transcriptions and translations, primarily those in Berlin as well as a group found near the German House in Luxor (https://dem-online.gwi.uni-muenchen.de/), while The Deir el-Medina Database (https://dmd.wepwawet.nl/) deals with the scholarly literature related to non-literary papyri and ostraca from the village. The latter is invaluable for anyone researching specific texts from the village, with search functions on names, titles, inventory numbers, and so on. Despite the narrow focus on this specific archaeological site, these two databases account for a substantial part of the surviving hieratic administrative documents of the New Kingdom. The literary material from the village has not been processed in the same way.

Other relevant digital resources include the online catalogues of individual museums, where many have now made their hieratic texts available as photographs online: the British Museum, Louvre, Ägyptisches Museum und Papyrussamlung in Berlin, Metropolitan Museum of Art, the Petrie Museum of Egyptian Archaeology, the Turin Papyrus Online Platform, to name just a few. Transliterations and translations of many hieratic texts can be found as part of the *Thesaurus Linguae Aegyptiae* (TLA: https://thesaurus-linguae-aegyptiae.de), and in Ramses Online (http://ramses.ulg.ac.be); the latter has a chronological focus on the New Kingdom which complements the Deir el-Medina databases by including texts from sites all over Egypt.

These resources are used regularly by specialists, but can profitably also be explored by others: the Deir el-Medina Database, for example, also includes a systematic bibliography of Deir el-Medina studies which allows for a different type of literature survey than the standard Online Egyptological Bibliography (http://oeb.griffith.ox.ac.uk).

7 Publication Practices

Hieratic manuscripts are normally published in a catalogue format, where the amount of information can vary significantly, as part of a synoptic edition of a specific composition, or as an individual edition of a specific manuscript such as a papyrus roll, an ostracon, or a writing board. The presentation and critical apparatus are rarely uniform, even if the basic principles are generally agreed upon: the goal is to provide an accurate version of a text in a format that is accessible to others, but also to record details of the materiality of a manuscript that might only be visible to someone who has worked with it first-hand (Quack, 2011). The 'craft' of text editing has changed less than most areas of Egyptology over the last 100 years, but it remains a core skill (Möschen, 2021: 1) and, given the number of unpublished hieratic manuscripts both in museums and from recent excavations, there is a real need for trained philologists.

7.1 Material Culture of Manuscripts

The basic physical aspects of manuscripts, such as size, colour, and state of preservation, have always been a fundamental part of an edition, but recent decades have seen a notable increase in the attention paid to the broader material culture of manuscripts. Part of this development is due to the theoretical insights of New or Material Philology, which emphasises the importance of looking at documents as archaeological artefacts in their own right. This has broad methodological implications for those working with primary sources, especially literary manuscripts. On the one hand, it highlights the need for close study of the production process: the activities of the scribe as copyist and editor, including careful or careless writing, his tendency to detect and correct errors, and his level of understanding of the text (Sections 3.5 and 4.4), but also the physical transmission of the document with signs of usage (patches on the back, for example) and traces of storage (dockets, insect damage). On the other hand, the prioritising of the study of individual literary manuscripts has equally important implications for their interpretation as more or less coherent copies of a given text: differences between copies are seen as evidence of human engagement with the text and its transmission, rather than simply data in a search for a mythical Ur-text through a list of scribal 'mistakes' (many of which turn out to be perfectly valid variants rather than errors). Several studies of the classics of the Egyptian literary tradition have used this methodology to reconstruct and recontextualise the compositions, resulting in an improved understanding of their role and importance (Geoga, 2021, 2022; Jurjens, 2021a, 2021b; Pries, 2022; Hagen, 2012; Parkinson, 2009).

7.2 Facsimiles and Photographs

In the early years of Egyptology, photographs were expensive to both take and print, and many publications of hieratic texts reproduced the script in facsimile drawings instead. This was not ideal because the ability to draw hieratic accurately is not simply a matter of faithfully reproducing what the eye can see, nor is it a matter of artistic talent. Recognising what one is looking at, which specific sign or group it is, and, last but not least, following the strokes of the original scribe, is crucial, and in that respect it is more a technical than artistic skill. Some of those who published early facsimiles could not read hieratic, and the quality of their drawings varied greatly, sometimes being so bad that it was difficult for even a specialist to read the text. Today, photographs are an indispensable part of the publication of a hieratic text, and – at least where two-dimensional objects like papyri are concerned – facsimile drawings less likely to be included. A partial exception to this is more three-dimensional objects like ostraca, where the uneven surface (occasionally with writing also on the edges) and faded or rubbed-off ink means that a facsimile drawing, based on photographs manipulated with imaging software (Section 8.2), as well as in-person investigation under different lighting conditions, can be very useful (Hagen, 2021: xiii). Such drawings allow for the inclusion of details that would not be visible in a published photograph (Burkard, Goecke-Bauer, & Wimmer, 2002: 202). Facsimiles are nonetheless subjective, and ironically those parts of a text where facsimiles are most reliable, that is, where the original hieratic is most visible and unproblematic, are also those parts where facsimiles are less useful. Where there are serious difficulties in reading, facsimiles can play an important role, but there they are also more likely to be impressionistic (Hagen, 2019a: 191). There is no absolute rule about the inclusion or otherwise of a facsimile drawing of a hieratic text in modern publications, and as an editor one must weigh the investment of time versus the potential value to colleagues; for example, will those interested be able to easily consult the original in the future? If a group of ostraca is destined for storage in an archaeological magazine in a rural area of Egypt, then the answer is probably no, and it is consequently worth taking the time to draw facsimiles.

7.3 Transcription, Translation, and Commentary

Although hieratic was the dominant script used by Egyptian scribes for a large part of Egyptian history, modern pedagogy has prioritised the teaching of hieroglyphs, and specifically texts written in the linguistic register of Middle Egyptian, to students. One of the implications of this is that there has long been a need to publish hieratic texts in transcription, which in English Egyptological terminology refers to the presentation of a hieratic text using hieroglyphs, in order to render the contents accessible to the majority of Egyptologists. This usage of the word transcription – as well as the subject-specific meaning of 'transliteration', which refers to the rendering in a latinised alphabet – may appear counter-intuitive to non-specialists (Burkard, Goecke-Bauer, & Wimmer, 2002: 199, n. 9), but it is by now well established. The resulting hieroglyphic text ideally communicates to the reader what signs the original hieratic text used, and although in many cases this is unproblematic (there is often a one-to-one correlation between a hieratic sign and a corresponding hieroglyph), the process can be complicated because of ligatures, damage to the manuscript, or ambiguously written signs (Figure 28). Many early publications of hieratic texts consisted solely of such transcriptions and an identification of content (a specific literary text, an account, a letter), with no further translation or commentary (Burkard, Goecke-Bauer, & Wimmer, 2002), perhaps partly because this would have involved extra work, and partly because it was assumed that most readers would be trained in hieroglyphs to such a level that it was unnecessary. The long-running catalogue of hieratic ostraca in the French Institute in Cairo, for example, was one of the first to include translations in 2000 (Grandet, 2000). This historical lack of translations has had the unfortunate effect that a significant number of texts in older publications, particularly ostraca, have not yet been made accessible to non-specialists.

Lithographically printed hieroglyphic texts have existed since the time of Champollion (Cherpion, 2012), and although metal letterpress sets for hieroglyphs were developed by the middle of the nineteenth century, for generations it remained more common to draw them by hand, partly because it was difficult to capture texts accurately otherwise (Scalf & Flannery, 2019).[8] As a result of this the majority of hieratic texts are primarily available in hieroglyphic transcriptions based on hand-copies. Since at least the mid 1980s, Egyptology has slowly made the transition to computer-generated hieroglyphs using a variety of software programs (Gozzoli, 2013: 90–96), of which the most widely used one today is probably Serge Rosmorduc's free JSESH (https://jsesh.qenherkhopeshef.org/). In addition to an intuitive and user-friendly interface with a wide range of signs, and the ability to manipulate signs with a lot of flexibility, this program also provides a group of signs for mimicking certain peculiarities of the hieratic script, including dots, curved strokes, and ditto marks. Alongside such specialised programs, Unicode is continually developing, and its repertoire of Egyptian hieroglyphs, as well as control characters to enable specific layouts, is expanding. This can facilitate the production and transfer of less elaborate sections of hieroglyphic text between documents and databases, but encoding hieroglyphs in Unicode is unlikely to replace dedicated programs like JSESH for the production of longer and more complex hieroglyphic texts for printed formats.

Historically there have been two Egyptological views on how hieratic should be transcribed into hieroglyphs: one early school of thought preferred to transcribe a hieratic sign with whatever hieroglyphic sign would be appropriate in a contemporary hieroglyph text (e.g. *nṯr*, 'god', as ⟨sign⟩), while a later school preferred whatever hieroglyphic sign corresponded to the actual sign used in the hieratic text (*nṯr*, 'god', as ⟨sign⟩). Today, most scholars adopt the guidelines proposed by Sir Alan H. Gardiner (1929; cf. Faulkner, 1935), who argued for the latter, and this seems also to be in line with the ancient Egyptian view, which held that the two scripts had separate orthographic traditions (Figure 26; cf. Fischer-Elfert, 2021: II, 347–353).

A hieroglyphic transcription can also disguise the variation of the original hieratic. A single hieroglyphic sign can sometimes be represented by two

---

[8] As a historical curiosity, there were early attempts at producing a standardised font for hieratic too, although it seems like it was only ever used for a single publication, namely the catalogue of papyri from the Museo Egizio in Turin (Pleyte & Rossi, 1869–1876; cf. Fischer-Elfert, 2021: I, 40–43). The amount of information lost by such standardisation was felt to be too high a cost (all hands look the same, and palaeographical dating becomes impossible), and the font was not adopted by others.

quite different hieratic signs, for example: the hieroglyph for *m* (𓅓) exists both as a full form (𓅓) and a more abbreviated form (𓏭), often used side by side in a single manuscript by a single scribe. Hieratic signs are, as a rule, simpler in form than their hieroglyphic counterparts, but simplicity does not in itself impair legibility, and there are cases where a hieratic sign is more distinct than the corresponding hieroglyph: a case in point is the bird-sign *tiw* (𓅂), which in the hieroglyphic script strongly resembles the bird-sign *ꜣ* (𓄿), but where the hieratic signs are much easier to distinguish from each other (𓅂 vs. 𓄿). Conversely, there are instances where a hieratic sign may represent several different hieroglyphs: the sign ⟩ can, for example, represent the hieroglyphs ⌒, ◠, ▭, or ▬, and the sign ↝ could in principle stand for ⌇, ⌢, ─, or ∩∩∩. In practice, understanding is often unproblematic as the syntax, phonetic complements, and the general context are enough to signal which sign is meant (see, however, Figure 28); as with demotic, 'as long as one looks at the complete word, most ambiguities are solved and there is only one possible interpretation' (Quack, 2010b: 249).

Alongside the hieroglyphic transcription, a modern editor will usually also provide a transliteration using a system based on the Latin alphabet, with a few extra signs from Semitic philology (e.g. *ꜣ* for aleph, *ꜥ* for ayin), that originally represented Egyptologists' understanding of the phonetic values of hieroglyphs. Historically there have been several systems in use, and even today there are a few different versions employed – a meeting of the International Association of Egyptologists agreed on a basic version in Leiden in 2023 – but what most of them have in common is that they make no attempt at accuracy in reflecting our current understanding of ancient Egyptian phonology: they are simply a convenient way for Egyptologists to convey linguistic information both in writing and verbally. The transliteration can communicate an editor's understanding of basic morphology, for example by showing roots separated typographically (e.g. with dots, n-dashes, or the equal sign) from endings or suffixes, by marking inflections, or indicating ancient omissions (see Figure 28 for an example of transliteration). Depending on the school of thought, this can also include signs that are not present in the original hieratic text but which the editor assumes, with greater or lesser confidence, were intended by the ancient scribe. Finally, a translation is normally provided, along with a brief commentary on grammar, lexicography, and interpretation/contextualisation.

Each of these steps involve multiple processes of interpretation: the translation is dependent on grammatical and lexicographic understanding, as well as context; the transliteration is dependent on the specific reading of hieroglyphic signs (some have several different phonetic values) and how syntax is understood; and finally the hieroglyphic transcription relies on the editor having recognised the hieratic signs correctly, a process which itself is closely linked to a holistic understanding of the contents. The latter is important to keep in mind for students and researchers alike: citing a hieratic text from a hieroglyphic transcription is already one step removed from the original. Figure 28 illustrates a case where one hieratic sign can be transcribed in two different ways, leading to two different translations.

A shipwrecked sailor returns home to Egypt bearing rich gifts, and is rewarded by the pharaoh:[9]

(a) $^c\!h^c.n$ $rdi.kw$ r $šmsw$, $s\underline{3}h.kw$ m $tp.w=f$
I was appointed as a Follower, and provided with **his/its servants**.

(b) $^c\!h^c.n$ $rdi.kw$ r $šmsw$, $s\underline{3}h.kw$ m $tp.w$ **200**
I was appointed as a Follower, and provided with **200 servants**.

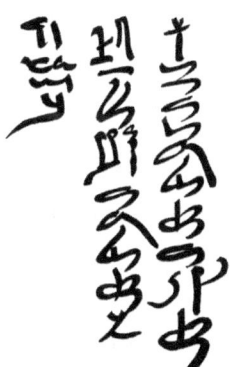

Figure 28 A facsimile drawing of columns 177–179 of *The Story of the Shipwrecked Sailor* (P. St. Petersburg 1115; partly restored for legibility). Drawing by F. Hagen.

---

[9] The hieratic text can be found in Golénischeff (1913), and the hieroglyphic transcription in Blackman (1932). As can be seen from the facsimile, this part of the papyrus is written in columns, but the transcription here has been adapted to a line format reading left to right for reasons of space.

The difference between the two versions is the reading of the final hieratic sign (𓂋), which looks like both the hieroglyph 𓂝 ('his') and the number 200 (𓏾). Both readings are palaeographically possible, make grammatical sense, and are contextually defensible, but the latter reading is now generally assumed to be correct, and is thought to represent an 'absurdly large' number in order to signal the 'fantastic nature of the story' (Allen, 2015: 49; Posener, 1976b: 146; for the former reading, see e.g. Lichtheim, 1975: 214). Such examples are in practice not very common, however, and most editions of hieratic texts have reasonably reliable transcriptions.

The possibility of online publication of high-resolution images offers opportunities for integrating transcriptions and translations with the visual nature of manuscripts as material artefacts, in a manner that goes some way towards addressing the abstraction created by the traditional methods of publication. An example of this is the website showcasing the famous Papyrus Prisse (https://prisse.ifao.egnet.net/), where users can click on any part of the manuscript and get a transcription, transliteration, and translation.

8 Future Perspectives

The application of digital technology to the analysis of hieratic texts is still in its infancy (Unter, 2025: 1–2), but progress in this field is likely to develop substantially in the coming decades. It is impossible to predict the ways in which this will happen, but even a brief overview of current projects demonstrates the potential of computer-assisted work on hieratic.

8.1 Machine-Learning, Automatic Translation, and Big Data Palaeography

The use of Optical Character Recognition (OCR) programs to 'read' hieratic texts, or more specifically to identify individual signs and groups of signs, is currently being explored. Research here has been promising (Bermeitinger, Gülden, & Konrad, 2021; Haliassos et al., 2020), and a recent contribution demonstrated the application of an OCR program to a specific dataset consisting of hieratic facsimiles of *The Story of the Shipwrecked Sailor* and *The Story of the Eloquent Peasant* (Tabin, 2023), with interesting results. Despite the inherent challenges of the hieratic script – the variations in forms of even a single sign are considerable, making automatic identification difficult, and ligatures and overlapping signs complicate matters further – this case study resulted in a correct identification in a random sample of signs of around 74 per cent at the lower end where the number of examples of signs for comparison are relatively few, but up to 95 per cent at the higher end for signs where comparative examples were more numerous. The project also formed the background for the Isut website (https://isut.uliege.be/signs/guesser), which among other functions has a 'guesser' where users can draw hieratic shapes that are then checked against its data, with outputs of suggestions for corresponding hieroglyphs. The underlying data are drawn from facsimiles of various papyrus manuscripts and is currently rather limited, but it showcases some of the potential of OCR.

One of the challenges that confronts any effort in this area is the limitation of the data: the low number of papyrus manuscripts and their often woeful state of survival (and, in the case of ostraca, the shortness of the texts) means that algorithms must be trained on fragmentary material. In addition, the format and nature of the hieratic text itself may be an issue, and it remains to be seen if programmes can handle images of papyri and ostraca as opposed to the facsimile drawings which have so far been used: Tabin (2023: 9) cautioned that such facsimiles 'will likely be the main source of additional data for the program's foreseeable future', which has obvious implications for its use. Until this hurdle can be overcome, and programmes can be taught to read 'contextually' (e.g. checking the plausibility of individual identifications based on signs before and after), it seems unlikely that computers will replace the work of human philologists, whether in terms of transcribing or translating hieratic texts, at least in the near future.

It will be clear from this discussion that the use of facsimiles as data for digital tools is becoming more prevalent, and this raises questions about the methodology of digital palaeographical drawing, as well as the need for accuracy (Gülden, Krause, & Verhoeven, 2020). Ideally the adoption of a standardised procedure would lead to consistency and more accurate facsimiles, but as Tabin (2023: 33–34) showed, 'facsimiles with lower accuracy can still be useful'. Direct work on digital photographs is also possible, and a recent project investigated the use of machine-learning methods to identify papyrus fragments belonging to specific manuscripts, by looking at a range of criteria such as colour, texture, line segmentation, and handwriting style, as well as content classification such as genre, with promising results (Unter, 2025).

8.2 Imaging Software

Traditionally philological work on hieratic texts has, at least ideally, been done in person by someone with direct access to the physical manuscripts, both because it allowed for an in-depth appreciation of the object as material culture (use-traces, physical properties, seeing it from all sides), and because it often resulted in better readings of faint traces. Today this hands-on approach is complemented by photography, which may help to detect traces that are no longer visible to the naked eye (Bülow-Jacobsen, 2020). In the early years of hieratic studies the expensive nature of photography precluded the inclusion of even black and white images, but as costs have come down it has become standard practice to include colour photographs (Section 7.2). One of the first photographic aids for philologists working with discoloured papyrus or faint ink was infrared photography, which could yield quite spectacular results, as in the case of carbonised papyri (Bülow-Jacobsen, 2008). Recent years have seen another breakthrough in imaging technology, or more correctly in imaging software. High-quality colour photographs can now be manipulated with various algorithms to enhance the visibility of ink traces, such as the D-Stretch software developed by Jon Harman, which has been particularly successful at bringing out red ink that in many cases is invisible to the naked eye. A similar program developed by the D-Scribes Project (directed by Isabelle Marthot-Santaniello) called Hierax – Software for Enhancing the Legibility of Papyri, is available for free (https://hierax.ch/) and allows for the output of numerous images from which the user can then choose, either for study or for publication (Atanasiu & Marthot-Santaniello, 2022). Such tools are a great practical help when deciphering fragmentary, dirty, and decayed manuscripts in the field, but also in the comfort of an office when preparing material for publication.

References

Allam, M. (2007). Die Kursivhieroglyphen: Sind sie Hieroglyphen oder Hieratisch? Zur Stellung der Kursivhieroglyphen innerhalb der ägyptischen Schriftgeschichte. *Annales du Service des Antiquités de l'Égypte,* 81, 33–37.

Allen, J. P. (2002). *The Hekanakht Papyri.* Publications of the Metropolitan Museum of Art Egyptian Expedition 27. New York: Metropolitan Museum of Art.

Allen, J. P. (2015). *Middle Egyptian Literature: Eight Literary Works of the Middle Kingdom.* Cambridge: Cambridge University Press.

Allon, N. (2023). The Social Lives of *mdw-nṯr*. *Hieroglyphs,* 1, 193–218.

Andreu-Lanoë, G. & Pelegrin, J. (2018). La fabrique des ostraca en calcaire: comment scribes et dessinateurs se procuraient-ils ces supports? In A. Dorn and S. Polis, eds., *Outside the Box: Selected Papers from the Conference "Deir el-Medina and the Theban Necropolis in Contact" Liège, 27–29 October 2014.* Liège: University of Liège Press, pp. 17–25.

Atanasiu, V. & Marthot-Santaniello, I. (2022). Legibility Enhancement of Papyri Using Color Processing and Visual Illusions: A Case Study in Critical Vision. *International Journal on Document Analysis and Recognition,* 25, 129–160.

Aufrère, S. H. (2009). Les alphabets dits « égyptiens » et « cophtes » de Fournier le Jeune (1766) et la « guerre des polices » au XVIIIe Siècle. In I. Regen and F. Servajean, eds., *Verba manent. Recueil d'études dédiées à Dimitri Meeks par ses collègues et amis.* Cahiers de l'ENiM 2. Montpellier: Université Paul Valéry (Montpellier III), pp. 29–49.

Baines, J. & Eyre, C. J. (2007). Four Notes on Literacy. In J. Baines, ed., *Visual and Written Culture in Ancient Egypt.* Oxford: Oxford University Press, pp. 63–94. [Revised version of an article published in *Göttinger Miszellen* 61 (1983), 65–96].

Barbotin, C. (2013). Les ostraca hiératiques de l'école du Ramesseum. *Memnonia,* 24, 73–79.

Barbotin, C. (2023). Les ostraca hiératiques et hiéroglyphiques de l'ecole du Ramesséum (Habilitation, Université de Lille). Available online at https://lilloa.univ-lille.fr/handle/20.500.12210/79416.

Barbotin, C. & Leblanc, C. (2023). *Le Ramesseum secteur sud-est (STO), l'école du temple. Description archéologique, catalogue des ostraca inscrits, catalogue des ostraca figurés.* Memnonia Cahier supplémentaire 3. Cairo: Dar el-Kutub.

Beinlich, H. (2017). *Der Mythos in seiner Landschaft – das ägyptische "Buch vom Fayum"*. Band 3: Die hieratisch-demotischen Texte. Studien zu den Ritualszenen altägyptischer Tempel 11.3. Dettelbach: J. H. Röll.

Bell, H. I., Nock, A. D., & Thompson, H. (1933). *Magical Texts from a Bilingual Papyrus in the British Museum*. London: Humphrey Milford Amen House.

Bell, M. R. (1990). Notes on the Exterior Construction Signs from Tutankhamun's Shrines. *Journal of Egyptian Archaeology*, 76, 107–124.

Van den Berg, H. & Donker van Heel, K. (2000). A Scribe's Cache from the Valley of the Queens? The Palaeography of Documents from Deir el-Medina: Some Remarks. In R. Demarée and A. Egberts, eds., *Deir el-Medina in the Third Millennium AD: A Tribute to Jac. J. Janssen*. Leiden: Nederlands Instituut voor het Nabije Oosten, pp. 9–49.

Bermeitinger, B., Gülden, S. A., & Konrad, T. (2021). How to Compute a Shape: Optical Character Recognition for Hieratic. In C. G. Zamacona und J. Ortiz-García, eds., *Handbook of Digital Egyptology. Texts*. Monografías Del Oriente Antiguo 1. Alcalá de Henares: Editorial Universidad de Alcalá, pp. 121–138.

Bickel, S. & Mathieu, B. (1993). L'écrivain Amennakht et son Enseignement. *Bulletin de l'institut français d'archéologie orientale*, 93, 31–51.

Blackman, A. M. (1932). *Middle Egyptian Stories*. Bibliotheca Aegyptiaca 2. Brussels: Fondation Égyptologique Reine Élisabeth.

Blackman, A. M. (1988). *The Story of King Kheops and the Magicians*. Edited for publication by W. V. Davies. Reading: J. V. Books.

Blasco Torres, A. I. (2015). Les ostraca de Narmouthis dans le contexte du bilinguisme gréco-égyptien de l'époque romaine. In G. Brun-Rigaud, ed., *Contacts, conflits, et créations linguistiques*. Paris: Éditions du Comtié des travaux historiques et scientifiques, pp. 11–18.

Von Bomhard, A. S. (1999). Le conte du Naufragé et le Papyrus Prisse. *Revue d'Égyptologie*, 50, 51–65.

Borchardt, L. (1907). Das Dienstgebäude des Auswärtigen Amtes unter den Ramessiden. *Zeitschrift für ägyptische Sprache und Altertumskunde*, 44, 59–61.

Boud'hors, A., et al. (2021). Les dépotoirs à tessons de Hout-Répit/Athribis et leur matériel inscrit. Rapport préliminaire (mission 2019–2020). *Bulletin de l'Institut français d'archéologie orientale*, 121, 69–145.

Brawanski, A. (2019). Die Schreiber des Papyrus Edwin Smith. In M. Brose et al. eds., *En détail: Philologie und Archäologie im Diskurs: Festschrift für Hans-Werner Fischer-Elfert*. Zeitschrift für Ägyptische

Sprache und Altertumskunde Beiheft 7. Berlin: De Gruyte, pp. 151–174.
Brunner, H. (1957). *Altägyptische Erziehung*, 2nd ed. Wiesbaden: Harrassowitz.
Buchwald, J. Z. & D. G. Josefowicz (2022). *The Riddle of the Rosetta. How an English Polymath and a French Polyglot Discovered the Meaning of Egyptian Hieroglyphs*. Princeton: Princeton University Press.
Bülow-Jacobsen, A. (2008). Infra-red Photography of Ostraca and Papyri. *Zeitschrift für Papyrologie und Epigraphik*, 165, 175–185.
Bülow-Jacobsen, A. (2020). Photography of Papyri and Ostraca. In C. Caputo and J. Lougovaya, eds., *Using Ostraca in the Ancient World: New Discoveries and Methodologies*. Materiale Textkulturen 32. Berlin: De Gruyter, pp. 59–86.
Burkard, G. (2013). Amunnakht, Scribe and Poet of Deir el-Medina: A Study of Ostracon O Berlin P 14262. In R. Enmarch and V. Lepper, eds., *Ancient Egyptian Literature: Theory and Practice*. Proceedings of the British Academy 188. Oxford: Oxford University Press, pp. 65–82.
Burkard, G., Goecke-Bauer, M., & Wimmer, S. (2002). Editing Hieratic Ostraca: Some Remarks for the New Centennium. In M. Eldamaty and M. Trad, eds., *Egyptian Museum Collections around the World: Studies for the Centennial of the Egyptian Museum, Cairo*. Vol. 1. Cairo: American University in Cairo Press, pp. 197–206.
Caminos, R. A. (1954). *Late-Egyptian Miscellanies*. Brown Egyptological Studies I. Oxford: Oxford University Press.
Caputo, C. (2019). Looking at the Material: One Hundred Years of Studying Ostraca from Egypt. In C. Ritter-Schmalz and R. Schwitter, eds., *Antike Texte und ihre Materialität: Alltägliche Präsenz, mediale Semantik, literarische Reflexion*. Berlin, Boston: De Gruyter, pp. 93–118.
Cavallo, G. (2011). Greek and Latin Writing in the Papyri. In R. S. Bagnall, ed., *The Oxford Handbook of Papyrology*. Oxford: Oxford University Press, pp. 101–148.
Černý, J. (1952). *Paper & Books in Ancient Egypt: An Inaugural Lecture Delivered at University College, 29 May 1947*. London: H. K. Lewis.
Černý, J. (1976). *Coptic Etymological Dictionary*. Cambridge: Cambridge University Press.
Chantrain, G. (2014). The Use of Classifiers in the New Kingdom. A Global Reorganization of the Classifiers System? *Lingua Aegyptiae*, 22, 39–59.
Chantrain, G. (2021). Classification Strategies from the End of the Ramesside Period until the Late Period: A Living System. *Zeitschrift für Ägyptische Sprache und Altertumskunde*, 148, 50–64.

Cherpion, N. (2012). *Le Dessinateur Cherubini et la Grammaire de Champollion*. Bibliothèque Générale 43. Cairo: Institut français d'archéologie orientale.

Christiansen, T. (2017). Manufacture of Black Ink in the Ancient Mediterranean. *Bulletin of the American Society of Papyrologists*, 54, 167–195.

Christiansen, T. et al. (2017). Chemical Characterization of Black and Red Inks Inscribed on Ancient Egyptian Papyri: The Tebtunis Temple Library. *Journal of Archaeological Science: Reports*, 14, 208–219.

Christiansen, T. et al. (2020). Insights into the Composition of Ancient Egyptian Red and Black Inks on Papyri Achieved by Synchrotron-based Microanalyses. *PNAS*, 117(45), 27825–27835.

Collombert, Ph. (2023). The Hieroglyphic Repertoire. In S. Polis, ed., *Guide to the Writing Systems of Ancient Egypt*. Cairo: Institut français d'archéologie orientale, pp. 126–132.

Cribiore, R. (2015). Literary Culture and Education in the Dakhla Oasis. In R. S. Bagnall et al., eds., *An Oasis City*. New York: New York University Press, pp. 179–192.

Darnell, J. C. (2013). *The Rock Shrine of Pahu, Gebel Akhenaton, and Other Rock Inscriptions from the Western Hinterland of Qamula*. Vol. II of *Theban Desert Road Survey*. Yale Egyptological Publications 1. Yale: Yale Egyptological Institute.

Darnell, J. C. & Darnell, D. (2002). *Gebel Tjauti Rock Inscriptions 1–45 and Wadi el-Hôl Rock Inscriptions 1–45*. Vol. I of *Theban Desert Road Survey in the Egyptian Western Desert*. Oriental Institute Publications 119. Chicago: Oriental Institute.

Davies, N. de G. (1943). *The Tomb of Rekhmire at Thebes*, 2 vols. The Metropolitan Museum of Art Egyptian Expedition 11. New York: Metropolitan Museum of Art.

Demarée, R. J. (with contributions by B. Leach and P. Usick). (2006). *The Bankes Late Ramesside Papyri*. London: British Museum Research Publication, 155.

Demarée, R. J. (2018). Some Notes on the Handwriting of the Scribe of the Tomb Dhutmose. In S. A. Gülden, K. Van Der Moezel, and U. Verhoeven, eds., *Ägyptologische "Binsen"-Weisheiten III. Formen und Funktionen von Zeichenliste und Paläographie. Akten der internationalen und interdisziplinären Tagung in der Akademie der Wissenschaften und der Literatur, Mainz im April 2016*. Einzelveröffentlichungen 15. Mainz: Akademie der Wissenschaften und der Literatur/Stuttgart: Franz Steiner Verlag, pp. 267–280.

Den Doncker, A. (2019). *Réactions aux images. Pour une réception des images en Égypte ancienne*. Unpublished PhD thesis, University of Leiden.

Den Doncker, A. (2023). Inscribing Objects. In S. Polis, ed., *Guide to the Writing Systems of Ancient Egypt*. Cairo: Institut français d'archéologie orientale, pp. 234–239.

Díaz-Iglesias Llanos, L. (2022). Hieratic Signs in a Cursive Hieroglyphic Text: The Case of the Burial Chamber of the Tomb of Djehuty (TT 11) with Additions of Other Contemporary Examples. In S. A. Gülden, T. Konrad, and U. Verhoeven, eds., *Ägyptologische "Binsen"-Weisheiten IV: Hieratisch des Neuen Reiches: Akteure, Formen und Funktionen. Akten der internationalen Tagung in der Akademie der Wissenschaften und der Literatur, Mainz im Dezember 2019*. Mainz: Akademie der Wissenschaften und der Literatur, pp. 127–154.

Díaz-Iglesias Llanos, L. (2023). Linear Hieroglyphs. In A. Stauder and W. Wendrich, eds., *UCLA Encyclopedia of Egyptology*. Los Angeles. https://escholarship.org/uc/item/2kz858gv.

Díaz-Iglesias Llanos, L. & Méndez-Rodríguez, D. M. (2023). Epigraphic Study of the Burial Chamber Belonging to Nakhtmin (TT 87): Materiality and Scribal Hands. *Journal of Near Easter Studies*, 82, 1–42.

Dieleman, J. (2005). *Priests, Tongues, and Rites: The London-Leiden Magical Manuscripts and Translation in Egyptian Ritual (100–300 CE)*. Religions in the Graeco-Roman World, 153. Leiden: Brill.

Donnat Beauquier, S. (2014). *Écrire à ses morts: Enquête sur un usage rituel de l'écrit dans l'Égypte pharaonique*. Grenoble: Jérôme Millon.

Donker van Heel, K. (2020). Some Issues in and Perhaps a New Methodology for Abnormal Hieratic. In V. Davies and D. Laboury, eds., *The Oxford Handbook of Egyptian Epigraphy and Palaeography*. Oxford: Oxford University Press, pp. 590–604.

Donker van Heel, K. & Haring, B. (2003). *Writing in a Workmen's Village: Scribal Practice in Ramesside Deir el-Medina*. Egyptologische Uitgaven 16. Leiden: Nederlands Instituut voor het Nabije Oosten.

Dorn, A. (2013). Kulturelle Topografie literarischer Texte. Versuch einer Funktions- und Bedeutungsbestimmung literarischer Texte im Mittleren Reich anhand ihrer archäologischen Kontexte. In G. Moers et al., eds., *Dating Egyptian Literary Texts*. Lingua Aegyptia Studia Monographica 11. Hamburg: Widmaier Verlag, pp. 73–109.

Dorn, A. (2015). Diachrone Veränderungen der Handschrift des Nekropolenschreibers Amunnacht, Sohn des Ipui. In U. Verhoeven, ed., *Ägyptologische "Binsen"-Weisheiten I–II. Neue Forschungen und*

Methoden der Hieratistik. Akten zweier Tagungen in Mainz im April 2011 und März 2013. Einzelveröffentlichungen 14. Mainz: Akademie der Wissenschaften und der Literatur/Stuttgart: Franz Steiner Verlag, pp. 175–218.

Dorn, A. (2022). Dating of literary ostraca with the Hieratische Paläographie der nicht-literarischen Ostraka der 19. und 20. Dynastie by Stefan Wimmer – an experiment. In S. Gülden, T. Konrad, and U. Verhoeven, eds., *Ägyptologische "Binsen"-Weisheiten IV*. Abhandlungen der Geistes- und sozialwissenschaftliche Klasse 17. Mainz: Akademie der Wissenschaften und der Literatur, pp. 155–383.

Dorn, A. (2023). Graffiti in Western Thebes Left by the Members of the Community of Workmen and Others: Past Research, Future Perspectives and a Recently Identified Eighteenth Dynasty Graffito. In B. G. Davies, ed., *Dispatches from Deir el-Medina*. Liverpool: Abercromby Press, pp. 91–108.

Dorn, A. & Polis, S. (2017). Nouveaux textes littéraires du scribe Amennakhte (et autres ostraca relatifs au scribe de la Tombe). *Bulletin de l'Institut français d'archéologie orientale*, 116, 57–96.

Dorn, A. & Polis, S. (2019). Le scribe de la Tombe Amennakhte: deux nouveau documents remarquables dans le fonds de l'Ifao. In F. Albert and A. Gasse, eds., *Études de documents hiératiques inédits – Travaux de la première Académie hiératiques*. Bibliothèque générale 56 / CENiM 22. Cairo: Institut français d'archéologie orientale, pp. 15–35.

Dorn, A. & Polis, S. (2022). The Hymn to Ptah as a Demiurgic and Fertility God on O. Turin CGT 57002: Contextualising an Autograph by Amennakhte Son of Ipuy. In S. Töpfer, P. del Vesco, and F. Poole, eds., *Deir el-Medina: Through the Kaleidoscope*. Turin: Museo Egizio, pp. 424–450.

Edel, E. (1980). *Die Felsgräbernekropole der Qubbet el Hawa bei Assuan, II. Abteilung: Die althieratischen Topfaufschriften. Paläographie der althieratischen Gefässaufschriften aus den Grabungsjahren 1960 bis 1973*. Abhandlungen der Rheinisch-Westfälischen Akademie der Wissenschaften 66. Wiesbaden: Harrassowitz.

El-Shahawy, A. (2010). *Recherche sur la décoration des tombes thébaines du Nouvel Empire*. Internet-Beiträge zur Ägyptologie und Sudanarchäologie XIII. London: Golden House Publications.

Enmarch, R. (2013). Some Literary Aspects of the Kamose Inscriptions. *Journal of Egyptian Archaeology*, 99, 253–263.

Enmarch, R. (2020). Paratextual Signs in Egyptian Texts of the Old and Middle Kingdoms. In N. Carlig et al., eds., *Signes dans les textes: Continuités et ruptures des pratiques scribales en Égypte pharaonique, gréco-romaine et byzantine*. Papyrologica Leodiensia 9. Liège: Presses Universitaires de Liège, pp. 41–56.

Erman, A. (1890). *Die Märchen des Papyrus Westcar*, 2 vols. Berlin: W. Spemann.

Erman, A. (1903). Zur Erklärung des Papyrus Harris. *Sitzungsberichte der Preußischen Akademie der Wissenschaften zu Berlin*, 21, 456–474.

Eyre, C. J. (2013). *The Use of Documents in Ancient Egypt*. Oxford: Oxford University Press.

Faulkner, R. O. (1935). Some Further Remarks on the Transcription of Late Hieratic. *Journal of Egyptian Archaeology*, 21, 49–51.

Firth, C. M. & Gunn, B. (1926). *Excavations at Saqqara: Teti Pyramid Cemeteries*, 2 vols. Cairo: Institut français d'archéologie orientale.

Fischer-Elfert, H.-W. (1986). *Die Satirische Streitschrift des Papyrus Anastasi I: Übersetzung und Kommentar*. Ägyptologische Abhandlungen 44. Wiesbaden: Harrassowitz.

Fischer-Elfert, H.-W. (2020). Hieratic Palaeography in Literary and Documentary Texts from Deir el-Medina. In V. Davies and D. Laboury, eds., *The Oxford Handbook of Egyptian Epigraphy and Palaeography*. Oxford: Oxford University Press, pp. 647–662.

Fischer-Elfert, H.-W. (2021). *Grundzüge einer Geschichte des Hieratischen*, 2 vols. Einführungen und Quellentexte zur Ägyptologie 14. Berlin: LIT Verlag.

Franke, D. (2013). *Egyptian Stelae in the British Museum from the 13th to 17th Dynasties*. Edited by M. Marée. London: British Museum Press.

Frood, E. (2007). *Biographical Texts from Ramesside Egypt*. Writings from the Ancient World 26. Atlanta: Society of Biblical Literature.

Galán, J. M. (2007). An Apprentice's Board from Dra Abu el-Naga. *Journal of Egyptian Archaeology*, 93, 95–116.

Gallo, P. (1997). *Ostraca demotici e ieratici dall'archivio bilingue di Narmouthis II*. Pisa: Edizioni ETS.

Gardiner, A. H. (1916). The Defeat of the Hyksos by Kamose: The Carnarvon Tablet, No. I. *Journal of Egyptian Archaeology*, 13, 95–110.

Gardiner, A. H. (1929). The Transcription of New Kingdom Hieratic. *Journal of Egyptian Archaeology*, 15, 48–55.

Gardiner, A. H. (1932). *Late-Egyptian Stories*. Bibliotheca Aegyptiaca 1. Brussels: Fondation Égyptologique Reine Élisabeth.

Gardiner, A. H. (1941). Ramesside Texts Relating to the Taxation and Transport of Corn. *Journal of Egyptian Archaeology*, 27, 19–73.

Gardiner, A. H. & Černý, J. (1957). *Hieratic Ostraca.* Vol. 1. Oxford: Griffith Institute.

Gasse, A. (1988). *Données nouvelles administratives et sacerdotales sur l'organisation du domaine d'Amon XXe-XXIe dynasties à la lumiére des papyrus Prachov, Reinhardt et Grundbuch (avec éditio princeps des papyrus Louvre AF 6345 et 6346–7).* Bibliothèque d'Étude 104, 2 vols. Cairo: Institut français d'archéologie orientale.

Gasse, A. (1992). Les ostraca hiératiques littéraires de Deir el-Medina: nouvelles orientations de la publication. In R. J. Demarée and A. Egberts, eds., *Village Voices: Proceedings of the Symposium "Texts from Deir el-Medîna and their interpretation," Leiden, May 31–June 1.* Leiden: Centre of Non-Western Studies, pp. 51–70.

Gasse, A. (2000). Le K2, un cas d'école? In R. J. Demarée and A. Egberts, eds., *Deir el-Medina in the Third Millenium AD: A Tribute to Jac. J. Janssen.* Egyptologische Uitgaven 14. Leiden: Nederlands Instituut voor het Nabije Oosten, pp. 109–120.

Gasse, A. (2005). *Catalogue des ostraca littéraires de Deir al-Médîna, V, Nos 1775–1873 et 1156.* Documents de fouilles de l'Institut français d'archéologie orientale 44. Cairo: Institut français d'archéologie orientale.

Gasse, A. (2016). Une caverne d'Ali Baba, la documentation hiératique des anciens Égyptiens. In L. Bazin Rizzo, A. Gasse, and F. Servajean, eds., *À l'école des scribes: Les écritures de l'Égypte Ancienne.* Les Cahiers Égypte Nilotique et Méditérranéenne 15. Montpellier: Silvana Editoriale, pp. 61–71.

Gasse, A. (2018). Les ligatures dans les textes hiératiques du Nouvel Empire (à partir des ostraca): Entre pragmatisme et maniérisme. In S. A. Gülden, K. Van Der Moezel, and U. Verhoeven, eds., *Ägyptologische "Binsen"-Weisheiten III. Formen und Funktionen von Zeichenliste und Paläographie. Akten der internationalen und interdisziplinären Tagung in der Akademie der Wissenschaften und der Literatur, Mainz im April 2016.* Einzelveröffentlichungen 15. Mainz: Akademie der Wissenschaften und der Literatur/Stuttgart: Franz Steiner Verlag, pp. 111–133.

Geoga, M. (2021). New Insights into Papyrus Millingen and the Reception History of The Teaching of Amenemhat. *Journal of Egyptian Archaeology,* 107, 225–238.

Geoga, M. (2022). Between Literature and History: Receptions of Poetry in Ancient Egypt. *Middle Eastern Literatures,* 25(2–3), 69–96.

Goedicke, H. (1988). *Old Hieratic Palaeography.* Baltimore: Halgo.

Golénischeff, W. (1913). *Les papyrus hiératiques nos. 1115, 1116A et 1116B de l'Ermitage Impérial à St. Petersbourg.* Leipzig: Harrassowitz.

Gozzoli, R. (2013). Hieroglyphic Text Processors, Manuel de Codage, Unicode, and Lexicography. In S. Polis and J. Winand, eds., *Texts, Languages & Information Technology in Egyptology.* Aegyptiaca Leodensia 9. Liège: Presses Universitaires de Liège, pp. 89–101.

Graefe, E. (2015). Über den parallelen Gebrauch von hieroglyphischen, kursivhieroglyphischen und hieratischen Schriftzeichen in Totentexten. In U. Verhoeven, ed., *Ägyptologische "Binsen"-Weisheiten I–II. Neue Forschungen und Methoden der Hieratistik. Akten zweier Tagungen in Mainz im April 2011 und März 2013* (Einzelveröffentlichungen 14). Mainz: Akademie der Wissenschaften und der Literatur/Stuttgart: Franz Steiner Verlag, pp. 119–142.

Grandet, P. (1994). *Le Papyrus Harris I*, 2 vols. Bibliothèque d'étude 109(1–2). Cairo: Institut français d'archéologie orientale.

Grandet, P. (2000). *Catalogue des ostraca hièratiques non littéraires de Deîr el-Médînéh VIII, Nos. 706-830.* Documents de fouilles de l'Institut français d'archéologie orientale 39. Cairo: Institut français d'archéologie orientale.

Grandet, P. (2023). Hieratic. In S. Polis, ed., *Guide to the Writing Systems of Ancient Egypt.* Cairo: Institut français d'archéologie orientale, pp. 62–69.

Grenfell, B. P., Hunt, A. S., & Goodspeed, E. J. (1907). *The Tebtunis Papyri, Part II.* Greco-Roman Memoirs 52. London: Egypt Exploration Society.

Griffith, F. Ll. & Petrie, W. M. F. (1889). *Two Hieroglyphic Papyri from Tanis.* London: Trübner & Co.

Gülden, S. A. (2016). Ein "nouveau Möller"? Grenzen und Möglichkeiten. Ein working paper zum gleichnamigen Vortrag. Hieratic Studies Online 1. Available online at https://aku.uni-mainz.de/hieratic-studies-online/.

Gülden, S. A. (2023a). Binsen, Bytes und Backups – Betrachtungen zum (Forschungs-) Datenmanagement im AKU-Projekt. In S. Gerhards et al., eds., *Schöne Denkmäler sind entstanden. Studien zu Ehren von Ursula Verhoeven.* Heidelberg: Propylaeum, pp. 133–150.

Gülden, S. A. (2023b). Studying Hieratic and Cursive Hieroglyphs in a Digital Age. In O. El-Aguizy and B. Kasparian, eds., *Proceedings of the Twelfth International Congress of Egyptologists, 3rd–8th November 2019, Cairo.* Bibliothèque Générale 71. Cairo: Institut français d'archéologie orientale, pp. 761–768.

Gülden, S. A., Krause, C., & Verhoeven, U. (2020). Digital Palaeography of Hieratic. In V. Davies and D. Laboury, eds., *The Oxford Handbook of Egyptian Epigraphy and Palaeography*. Oxford: Oxford University Press, pp. 634–646.

Habachi, L. 1972. *The Second Stela of Kamose and His Struggle Against the Hyksos Ruler and his Capital*. Abhandlungen des Deutschen Archäologischen Instituts Kairo 8. Glückstadt: J. J. Augustin.

Hagen, F. (2011). The Hieratic Dockets on the Cuneiform Tablets from Amarna. *Journal of Egyptian Archaeology*, 97, 214–216.

Hagen, F. (2012). *An Ancient Egyptian Literary Text in Context: The Instruction of Ptahhotep*. Orientalia Lovaniensia Analecta 218. Leuven: Peeters.

Hagen, F. (2013). An Eighteenth Dynasty Writing Board (Ashmolean 1948.91) and the Hymn to the Nile. *Journal of the American Research Center in Egypt*, 49, 73–91.

Hagen, F. (2016). On Some Movements of the Royal Court in New Kingdom Egypt. In J. van Dijk, ed., *Another Mouthful of Dust: Egyptological Studies in Honour of Geoffrey Thorndike Martin*. Orientalia Lovaniensia Analecta 246. Leuven: Peeters, pp. 155–182.

Hagen, F. (with a contribution by D. Soliman). (2018). Archives in Ancient Egypt, 2500–1000 BCE. In A. Bausi et al., eds., *Manuscripts and Archives: Comparative Views on Record-Keeping*. Studies in Manuscript Cultures 11. Berlin, Boston: De Gruyter, pp. 71–170.

Hagen, F. (2019a). New Copies of Old Classics: Early Manuscripts of Khakheperreseneb and The Instruction of a Man for His Son. *Journal of Egyptian Archaeology*, 105, 177–208.

Hagen, F. (2019b). Libraries in Ancient Egypt, 1500–1000 BC. In K. Ryholt and G. Barjamovic, eds., *Libraries before Alexandria: Ancient Near Eastern Traditions*. Oxford: Oxford University Press, pp. 244–318.

Hagen, F. (2021). *Ostraca from the Temple of a Million Years of Thutmose III*. Culture and History of the Ancient Near East 120. Leiden: Brill.

Hagen, F. (2024). The Hieratic Material from the Temple of a Million Years of Thutmose III: A Preliminary Report. In M. Seco Álvarez and J. Martínez Babón, eds., *A Place of Worship and Burial: The Site of the Temple of Millions of Years of Thutmose III in Thebes*. Sevilla: Editorial Universidad de Sevilla, pp. 171–202.

Hagen, F. & Ryholt, K. (2016). *The Antiquities Trade in Egypt 1880–1930: The H. O. Lange Papers*. Scientia Danica. Series H. Humanistica, 4. Vol. 8. Copenhagen: Det Kongelige Danske Videnskabernes Selskab.

Haliassos, A. et al. (2020). Classification and Detection of Symbols in Ancient Papyri. In F. Liarokapis et al., eds., *Visual Computing for Cultural Heritage*. Cham: Springer International Publishing, pp. 121–140. https://doi.org/10.1007/978-3-030-37191-3_7.

Haring, B. (1997). *Divine Households: Administrative and Economic Aspects of the New Kingdom Royal Memorial Temples in Western Thebes*. Egyptologische Uitgaven 12. Leiden: Nederlands Instituut voor het Nabije Oosten.

Haring, B. (2015). Hieratic Drafts for Hieroglyphic Texts? In U. Verhoeven, ed., *Ägyptologische "Binsen"-Weisheiten I–II. Neue Forschungen und Methoden der Hieratistik. Akten zweier Tagungen in Mainz im April 2011 und März 2013* (Einzelveröffentlichungen 14). Mainz: Akademie der Wissenschaften und der Literatur/Stuttgart: Franz Steiner Verlag, pp. 67–84.

Haring, B. (2018). *From Single Sign to Pseudo-Script: An Ancient Egyptian System of Workmen's Marks*. Culture and History of the Ancient Near East 93. Leiden: Brill.

Haring, B. (2020). The Survival of Pharaonic Ostraca: Coincidence or Meaningful Patterns? In C. Caputo and J. Lougovaya, eds., *Using Ostraca in the Ancient World: New Discoveries and Methodologies*. Materiale Textkulturen 32. Berlin: De Gruyter, pp. 89–108.

Haring, B. (2023). *Hieroglyphs, Pseudo-Scripts and Alphabets: Their Use and Reception in Ancient Egypt and Neighbouring Regions*. Cambridge Elements – Ancient Egypt in Context. Cambridge: Cambridge University Press.

Haring, B. & Soliman, D. (2014). Reading Twentieth Dynasty Ostraca with Workmen's Marks. In B. Haring, O. Kaper, and R. van Walsem, eds., *The Workman's Progress: Studies in the Village of Deir el-Medina and documents from Western Thebes in Honour of Rob Demarée*. Egyptologische Uitgaven 28. Leuven: Peeters, pp. 73–93.

Hassan, Kh. (2014). A Visitor's Hieratic Ostracon Concerning the Temple of Deir el-Bahri. *Bulletin de l'Institut français d'archéologie orientale*, 113, 183–192.

Hassan, Kh. (2017). New Literary Compositions of the Scribe Amunnakhte Son of Ipuy. A Study of Hieratic Ostracon in the Egyptian Museum of Cairo. *Studien zur altägyptischen Kultur,* 46, 101–111.

Hassan, Kh. & Mekawy Ouda, M. (2018). Ramesside Hieratic Stela of the Sandal Maker Penone in the Egyptian Museum Cairo (TR. 27.6.24.3). *Journal of the American Research Center in Egypt,* 54, 93–105.

Hayes, W. C. (1959). *The Scepter of Egypt*, 2 vols. New York: The Metropolitan Museum of Art.

Helck, W. (1984). Zum Brooklyner Orakelpapyrus. In H.-J. Thissen and K-Th. Zauzich, eds., *Grammata Demotika: Festscgrift für Erich Lüddeckens*. Würzburg: Zauzich, pp. 71–74.

Hoch, J. E. (1994). *Semitic Words in Egyptian Texts of the New Kingdom and Third Intermediate Period*. Princeton, NJ: Princeton University Press.

Hornung, E. (1997). *Der ägyptische Mythos von der Himmelskuh: eine Ätiologie des Unvollkommenen*, 3rd ed. Orbis biblicus et orientalis 46. Freiburg: Universitätsverlag.

Izre'el, S. (1997). *The Amarna Scholarly Tablets*. Cuneiform Monographs 9. Leiden: Styx.

Izre'el, S. (2001). *Adapa and the South Wind Has the Power of Life and Death Mesopotamian Civilizations 10*. Winona Lake: Eisenbrauns.

Jäger, S. (2004). *Altägyptische Berufstypologien*. Lingua Aegyptia Studia Monographica 4. Göttingen: Seminar für Ägyptologie und Koptologie.

Jansen-Winkeln, K. (2017a). "Libyerzeit" oder "postimperiale Periode"? Zur historischen Einordnung der Dritten Zwischenzeit. In C. Jurman, B. Bader, and D. A. Aston, eds., *A True Scribe of Abydos: Essays on First Millennium Egypt in Honour of Anthony Leahy*. Orientalia Lovaniensia Analecta 265. Leuven: Peeters, pp. 203–238.

Jansen-Winkeln, K. (2017b). Review of A. Stauder, *Linguistic Dating of Middle Egyptian Literary Texts* and G. Moers et al. (eds.), *Dating Egyptian Literary Texts*. *Orientalia*, 86, 107–134.

Janssen, J. J. (1987). On Style in Egyptian Handwriting. *Journal of Egyptian Archaeology*, 73, 161–167.

Janssen, J. J. (1997). Review of S. Wimmer, *Hieratische Paläographie der nicht-literarischen Ostraka der 19. und 20. Dynastie (1995)*. *Bibliotheca Orientalis*, 54, 338–345.

Janssen, J. J. (2000). Idiosyncrasies in Late Ramesside Hieratic Writing. *Journal of Egyptian Archaeology*, 86, 51–56.

Jasnow, R. (1992). *A Late Period Hieratic Wisdom Text (P. Brooklyn 47.218.135)*. Studies in Ancient Oriental Civilization 52. Chicago: Oriental Institute.

Jüngling, J. (2021). *Hieratische Aktenvermerke*. Hieratic Studies Online 2. Mainz. Available online at https://aku.uni-mainz.de/hieratic-studies-online/.

Jurjens, J. (2021a). The Educational Context of a Literary Text: Some Notes on Marginalia and Drawings as Found on Material Containing The Teaching of Khety. *Journal of the American Research Center in Egypt,* 57, 175–196.

Jurjens, J. (2021b). An Unpublished Manuscript of The Teaching of Khety (P. Turin CGT 54019). *Rivista del Museo Egizio,* 5, 109–128.

Jurjens, J. (2024). *The Teaching of Khety & Its Use as an Educational Tool in Ancient Egypt.* Unpublished PhD thesis, University of Leiden.

Kahl, J. (2010). Archaism. *UCLA Encyclopedia of Egyptology.* Available online at https://escholarship.org/uc/item/3tn7q1pf.

Kaper, O. (2010). A Kemyt ostracon from Amheida, Dakhleh Oasis. *Bulletin de l'Institut français d'archéologie orientale,* 110, 115–126.

Kitchen, K. A. (1969–1990). *Ramesside Inscriptions, Historical and Biographical,* 8 vols. Oxford: Blackwells.

Konrad, T. (2023). Cursive Hieroglyphs. In S. Polis, ed., *Guide to the Writing Systems of Ancient Egypt.* Cairo: Institut français d'archéologie orientale, pp. 58–61.

Krutzsch, M. (2017). Einzelblatt und Rolle: zur Anatomie von Papyrushandschriften. In F. Feder, G. Sperveslage, and F. Steinborn, eds., *Ägypten begreifen: Erika Endesfelder in memoriam,* Internet-Beiträge zur Ägyptologie und Sudanarchäologie 19. London: Golden House, pp. 213–222.

Krutzsch, M. (2019). Erkenntnisse und Fragen zum Schriftträger Papyrus. In M. Brose, P. Dils, F. Naether, L. Popko, and D. Raue, eds., *En détail – Philologie und Archäologie im Diskurs: Festschrift für Hans-Werner Fischer-Elfert 1.* Berlin: De Gruyter, pp. 503–513.

Kurth, D. (1999). Der Einfluss der Kursive auf die Inschriften des Tempels von Edfu. In D. Kurth, ed., *Edfu. Bericht über drei Surveys: Materialen und Studien.* Die Inschriften des Tempels von Edfu, Begleitheft 5. Wiesbaden: Harrassowitz, pp. 69–96.

Laboury, D. (2017). Tradition and Creativity: Toward a Study of Intericonicity in Ancient Egyptian Art. In T. Gillen, ed., *(Re)productive Traditions in Ancient Egypt: Proceedings of the Conference held at the University of Liège 6th–8th February 2013.* Aegyptiaca Leodensia 10. Liège: Presses Universitaires de Liège, pp. 229–258.

Laboury, D. (2022). Artistes et écriture hiéroglyphique dans l'Égypte des pharaons. *Bulletin de la Societé française d'égyptologie,* 207, 37–68.

Lacau, P. (1939). Une stèle du roi "Kamosis". *Annales du service des antiquités de l'Égypte,* 39, 245–271.

Landrino, M. (In preparation). *Hieratische Chrestomathie II: The New Kingdom*. Berlin: LIT Verlag.

Lange, E. (2007). Kretischer Zauber gegen asiatischen Seuchen: Die kretischen Zaubersprüche in den altägyptischen medizinischen Texten. In R. Hannig, P. Vomberg, and O. Witthuhn, eds., *Marburger Treffen zur altägyptischen Medizin. Vorträge und Ergebnisse 2002–2007*. Göttinger Miszellen Beihefte 2. Göttingen: Seminar für Ägyptologie und Koptologie, pp. 47–55.

Lange, H. O. & Schäfer, H. (1908). *Grab- und Denksteine des Mittleren Reichs, No. 20001–20780*. Berlin: Reichsdruckerei.

Lazaridis, N. (2010). Education and Apprenticeship. *UCLA Encyclopedia of Egyptology*. Available online at https://escholarship.org/uc/item/1026h44g.

Leblanc, C. (2004). L'école du temple (ât-sebait) et le per-ankh (maison de vie). Á propos de récentes découvertes effectuées dans le contexte du Ramesseum. *Memnonia*, 15, 93–101.

Leitz, C. (1999). *The Magical and Medical Papyri of the New Kingdom*. Hieratic Papyri in the British Museum VII. London: British Museum Press.

Lenzo Marchese, G. (2004). Les colophons dans la littérature égyptienne. *Bulletin de l'Institut français d'archéologie orientale*, 104, 359–376.

Lenzo Marchese, G. (2015). L'écriture hiératique en épigraphie à l'époque napatéenne. In U. Verhoeven, ed., *Ägyptologische "Binsen"-Weisheiten I–II. Neue Forschungen und Methoden der Hieratistik. Akten zweier Tagungen in Mainz im April 2011 und März 2013*. Einzelveröffentlichungen 14. Mainz: Akademie der Wissenschaften und der Literatur/Stuttgart: Franz Steiner Verlag, pp. 271–295.

Lenzo Marchese, G. (2023). The Book of the Dead in the Third Intermediate Period. In R. Lucarelli and M. A. Stadler, eds., *The Oxford Handbook of the Egyptian Book of the Dead*. Oxford: Oxford University Press, pp. 76–115.

Lepper, V. (2008). *Untersuchungen zu pWestcar: Eine philologische und literaturwissenschaftliche (Neu-)analyse*. Ägyptologische Abhandlungen 70. Wiesbaden: Harrassowitz.

Lichtheim, M. (1975). *Ancient Egyptian Literature, Volume I: The Old and Middle Kingdom*. Berkeley: University of California Press.

Lieven, A. von. (2007). *Grundriss der Laufes der Sterne: Das sogenannte Nutbuch*. The Carlsberg Papyri 8. CNI Publications 31. Copenhagen: Museum Tusculanum Press.

Lieven, A. von & Quack, J. F. (2018). Ist Lieben eine Frauenkrankheit? Papyrus Berlin P 13602, ein gynäkomagisches Handbuch. In K.

Donker van Heel, F. A. J. Hoogendijk, and C. J. Martin, eds., *Hieratic, Demotic and Greek Studies and Text Editions. Of Making Many Books There Is No End: Festschrift in Honour of Sven P. Vleeming*. Papyrologica Lugduno-Batava 34. Leiden: Brill, pp. 257–274.

López, J. (1980). *Ostraca ieratici*, vol. II: n. 57093–57319. Catalogo del Museo Egizio di Torino Serie II, Collezioni 3/2. Milan: Cisalpino Goliardica.

Lucarelli, R. (2020). Cursive Hieroglyphs in the Book of the Dead. In V. Davies and D. Laboury, eds., *The Oxford Handbook of Egyptian Epigraphy and Palaeography*. Oxford: Oxford University Press, pp. 577–589.

Luiselli, M. (2003). The Colophons as an Indication of the Attitudes towards the Literary Tradition in Egypt and Mesopotamia. In S. Bickel and A. Loprieno, eds., *Basel Egyptology Prize 1: Junior Research in Egyptian History, Archaeology, and Philology*. Aegyptiaca Helvetica 17. Basel: Schwabe, pp. 343–360.

Lüscher, B. (2015). Kursivhieroglyphische Ostraka als Textvorlagen: Der (Glücks-)Fall TT 87. In U. Verhoeven, ed., *Ägyptologische "Binsen"-Weisheiten I–II. Neue Forschungen und Methoden der Hieratistik. Akten zweier Tagungen in Mainz im April 2011 und März 2013*. Einzelveröffentlichungen 14. Mainz: Akademie der Wissenschaften und der Literatur/Stuttgart: Franz Steiner Verlag, pp. 85–117.

Lüscher, B. (2017). Papyrus Paris, Bibliothèque Nationale 46: ein Beitrag zur frühen Rezeptionsgeschichte des Totenbuches. In S. Bickel and L. Díaz-Iglesias, eds., *Studies in Ancient Egyptian Funerary Literature*. Orientalia Lovaniensia Analecta 257. Leuven: Peeters, pp. 355–374.

Mathieu, B. (2003). La littérature égyptienne sous les Ramsès d'après les ostraca littéraires de Deir el-Médineh. In G. Andreu, ed., *Deir el-Médineh et la Vallée des Rois: la vie en Égypte au temps des pharaons du Nouvel Empire*. Paris: Khéops, pp. 117–137.

McClain, S. E. (2018). Authorship and Attribution: Who Wrote the Twentieth Dynasty Journal of the Necropolis? In A. Dorn and S. Polis, eds., *Outside the Box: Selected Papers from the Conference 'Deir el-Medina and the Theban Necropolis in Contact', Liège, 27–29 October 2014*. Aegyptiaca Leodiensia 11. Liège: University of Liège Press, pp. 333–364.

McDowell, A. (2000). Teachers and Students at Deir el-Medina. In R. J. Demarée and A. Egberts, eds., *Deir el-Medina in the Third Millenium AD: A Tribute to Jac. J. Janssen*. Leiden: Nederlands Instituut voor het Nabije Oosten, pp. 217–233.

Meeks, D. (2007). La paléographie hiéroglyphique: une discipline nouvelle. *Égypte, Afrique et Orient*, 46, 3–14.

Megally, M. (1971). *Considérations sur les variations et la transformation des formes hiératiques du Papyrus E 3236 du Louvre*. Bibliothèque d'étude 49. Cairo: Institut français d'archéologie orientale.

Messerer, C. (2017). *Corpus des papyrus grecs sur les relations administratives entre le clergé égyptien et les autorités romaines*. Vol. 1. Sonderreihe der Abhandlungen Papyrologica Coloniensia 41. Leiden: Brill.

Miyanishi, M. (2016). *Palaeographical Study of the Late Ramesside Letters Vol. I & II*. Unpublished PhD thesis, University of Liverpool. Available online at https://livrepository.liverpool.ac.uk/id/eprint/3002144.

Moers, G. et al., eds., (2013). *Dating Egyptian Literary Texts*. Linguae Aegyptiae Studia Monographica 11. Hamburg: Widmaier Verlag.

Moezel, K. van der. (2022). *Administrative Hieratic from dynasties 19 and 20: Case studies on selected groups of ostraca with necropolis administration*. Hieratic Studies Online 4. Mainz. http://doi.org/10.25358/openscience-7839.

Möller, G. (1910). Das Dekret des Amenophis, des Sohnes des Hapu. *Sitzungsberichte der Königlich Preussischen Akademie der Wissenschaften zu Berlin*, XLVII, 932–948, pl. VI.

Möller, G. (1920). Zur Datierung literarischer Handschriften aus der ersten Hälfte des Neuen Reiches. *Zeitschrift für Ägyptische Sprache und Altertumskunde*, 56, 34–43.

Möller, G. (1927–35). *Hieratische Lesestücke für den akademischen Gebrauch*, 3 vols. Leipzig: J. C. Hinrich'sche Buchhandlung.

Möller, G. (1927–36). *Hieratische Paläographie: Die aegyptische Buchschrift in ihrer Entwicklung von der fünften Dynastie bis zur römischen Kaiserzeit*, 3 vols. Leipzig: J. C. Hinrich'sche Buchhandlung.

Morfini, I. (2019). *Necropolis Journal: Daily Records of Events in an Ancient Egyptian Artisans' Community*. Unpublished PhD thesis, University of Leiden. Available online at https://hdl.handle.net/1887/68810.

Morris, R. (2021). *Forensic Handwriting Identification: Fundamental Concepts and Principles*, 2nd ed. London: Academic Press, Elsevier.

Möschen, S. (2021). *Hieratische Chrestomathie, Teil I: Altes und Mittleres Reich*. Einführungen und Quellentexte zur Ägyptologie 15. Berlin: Lit Verlag.

Motte, A. (2022). Kemit, Writing-boards, and Palaeographic Studies. In S. Gülden, T. Konrad, and U. Verhoeven, eds., *Ägyptologische*

"Binsen"-Weisheiten IV. Abhandlungen der Geistes- und sozialwissenschaftliche Klasse 17. Mainz: Akademie der Wissenschaften und der Literatur, pp. 341–383.

Motte, A. (2024). Learning Through Practice: On How Kemyt Contributed to Crafting and Transmitting Scribal Knowledge. *Zeitschrift für Ägyptische Sprache und Altertumskunde*, 151, 92–109.

Motte, A. & Sojic, N. (2020). Paratextual Signs in the New Kingdom Medico-magical Texts. In N. Carlig et al., eds., *Signes dans les textes: Continuités et ruptures des pratiques scribales en Égypte pharaonique, gréco-romaine et byzantine*. Papyrologica Leodiensia 9. Liège: Presses Universitaires de Liège, pp. 57–94.

Munro, I. (1994). *Die Totenbuch-Handschriften der 18. Dynastie im Ägyptischen Museum Cairo*, 2 vols. Ägyptologische Abhandlungen 54. Wiesbaden: Harrassowitz.

Navratilova, H. (2015). *Visitor's Graffiti of Dynasties 18 and 19 in Abusir and Northern Saqqara*, 2nd ed. Liverpool: Abercromby Press.

Ormont, H. (1902). *Missions archéologique françaises en orient aux XVII et XVIII siècles*, 2 vols. Paris: Imprimerie nationale.

Osing, J. & Rosati, G. (1998). *Papiri geroglifici e ieratici da Tebtynis*, 2 vols. Florence: Istituto Papirologico "G. Vitelli".

Pantalacci, L. (2018). Between Old and Middle Kingdom: Palaeography of the Clay Documents from Bala. In S. A. Gülden, K. Van Der Moezel, and U. Verhoeven, eds., *Ägyptologische "Binsen"-Weisheiten III. Formen und Funktionen von Zeichenliste und Paläographie. Akten der internationalen und interdisziplinären Tagung in der Akademie der Wissenschaften und der Literatur, Mainz im April 2016*. Einzelveröffentlichungen 15. Mainz: Akademie der Wissenschaften und der Literatur/Stuttgart: Franz Steiner Verlag, pp. 217–234.

Pantalacci, L. (2021). Writing on Clay: Documentation from Balat (Dakhla Oasis, End of the 3rd Millennium). In Ph. Collombert and P. Tallet, eds., *Les archives administratives de l'Ancien Empire*. Leuven: Peeters, pp. 297–310.

Parker, R. A. (1962). *A Saite Oracle Papyrus from Thebes in the Brooklyn Museum [Papyrus Brooklyn 47.218.3]*. Providence, Rhode Island: Brown University Press.

Parkinson, R. B. (1999). *Cracking Codes: The Rosetta Stone and Decipherment*. Berkeley: University of California Press.

Parkinson, R. B. (2004). The History of a Poem: Middle Kingdom Literary Manuscripts and their Reception. In G. Burkard, A. Grimm, S. Schoske, A. Verbovsek, eds., *Kon-Texte: Akten des Symposions*

"Spurensuche – Altägypten im Spiegel seiner Texte" München 2. bis 4. Mai 2003. Ägypten und Altes Testament 60. Wiesbaden: Harrassowitz, pp. 51–64.

Parkinson, R. B. (2009). *Reading Ancient Egyptian Poetry: Among Other Histories*. Chichester: Wiley-Blackwell.

Parkinson, R. B. (2013). Sailing Past Elsinore. Interpreting the Materiality of Middle Kingdom Poetry. In G. Moers et al., eds., *Dating Egyptian Literary Texts*. Lingua Aegyptia Studia Monographica 11. Hamburg: Widmaier Verlag, pp. 123–137.

Parkinson, R. B. (2019). Libraries in Ancient Egypt, c.2600–1600 BCE. In K. Ryholt and G. Barjamovic, eds., *Libraries before Alexandria: Ancient Near Eastern Traditions*. Oxford: Oxford University Press, pp. 115–167.

Parkinson, R. B. & Quirke, S. (1995). *Papyrus*. London: British Museum Press.

Parkinson, R. B. & Spencer, N. (2017). The Teaching of Amenemhat at Amara West: Egyptian Literary Culture in Upper Nubia. In N. Spencer, A. Stevens, and M. Binder, eds., *Nubia in the New Kingdom: Lived Experience, Pharaonic Control and Indigenous Traditions*. British Museum Studies on Egypt and Sudan 3. Leuven: Peeters, pp. 214–223.

Peden, A. J. (2001). *The Graffiti of Pharaonic Egypt: Scope and Roles of Informal Writings (c. 3100–332 BC)*. Probleme der Ägyptologie 17. Leiden: Brill.

Pelegrin, J., G. Andreu-Lanoë, & C. Pariselle (2016). La production des ostraca en calcaire dans la nécropole thébaine: étude préliminaire. *Bulletin de l'Institut Français d'Archéologie Orientale*, 115, 325–352.

Pleyte, W. & Rossi, F. (1869–1876). *Les papyrus hiératiques de Turin*, 2 vols. Leiden: Brill.

Polis, S. (2017a). Linguistic Variation in Ancient Egyptian: An Introduction to the State of the Art (with Special Attention to the Community of Deir el-Medina). In J. Cromwell and E. Grossman, eds., *Scribal Repertoires in Egypt from the New Kingdom to the Early Islamic Period*. Oxford: Oxford University Press, pp. 60–88.

Polis, S. (2017b). The Scribal Repertoire of Amennakhte Son of Ipuy. Describing Variation across Late Egyptian Registers. In J. Cromwell and E. Grossman, eds., *Scribal Repertoires in Egypt from the New Kingdom to the Early Islamic Period*. Oxford: Oxford University Press, pp. 89–126.

Polis, S. (2020). Methods, Tools, and Perspectives of Hieratic Palaeography. In V. Davies and D. Laboury, eds., *The Oxford Handbook of Egyptian Epigraphy and Palaeography*. Oxford: Oxford University Press, pp. 550–565.

Polis, S. (2022). The Messy Scribe from Deir el-Medina. A Paleographical Journey through the Texts of a Draughtsman and Scribe from the 19th Dynasty: Pay (i). In S. A. Gülden, T. Konrad, and U. Verhoeven, eds., *Ägyptologische "Binsen"-Weisheiten IV. Hieratisch des Neuen Reiches: Akteure, Formen und Funktionen. Akten der internationalen Tagung in der Akademie der Wissenschaften und der Literatur, Mainz im Dezember 2019.* Einzelveröffentlichungen 17. Mainz: Akademie der Wissenschaften und der Literatur/Stuttgart: Franz Steiner Verlag, pp. 405–453.

Polis, S. & Seyr, Ph. (2023). Enigmatic Texts from Deir el-Medina. On the Transmission and Decipherment of "cryptographic" Compositions in the Community of Workmen. *Revue d'Égyptologie,* 73, 117–182.

Popko, L. (2016). Die hieratische Stele MAA 1939.552 aus Amara West: ein neuer Feldzug gegen die Philister. *Zeitschrift für ägyptische Sprache und Altertumskunde,* 143, 214–233.

Posener, G. (1951a). *Catalogue des ostraca hiératiques littéraires de Deir el Médineh, II, Nos. 1109–1266.* Documents de fouilles de l'Institut français d'archéologie orientale 18. Cairo: Institut français d'archéologie orientale.

Posener, G. (1951b). Sur l'emploi de l'encre rouge dans les manuscrits égyptiens. *Journal of Egyptian Archaeology,* 37, 75–80.

Posener, G. (1957). Le conte de Néferkarê et du général Siséné (recherches littéraires, VI). *Revue d'Égyptologie,* 11, 119–137.

Posener, G. (1972). Champollion et le déchiffrement de l'écriture hiératique. *Comptes rendus des séances de l'Academie des Inscriptions et Belles-Lettres,* 116e année, 3, 566–573.

Posener, G. (1975). Les ostraca numérotés et le conte du revenant. In *Drevnii Vostok: sbornik 1* (Festschrift Korostovstev). Moscow: 'Nauka', pp. 105–112.

Posener, G. (1976a). *L'Ensignement loyaliste: sagesse égyptienne du Moyen Empire.* Centre de Recherches d'Histoire et de Philologie II, Hautes études orientales 5. Geneva: Droz.

Posener, G. (1976b). Notes de transcription. *Revue d'égyptologie,* 28, 146–148.

Prada, L. (2018). Egyptian Education in Hellenistic and Roman Egypt: A Take from the Fayum – School Textbooks and *P. Schulübung* Revisited. In M.-P. Chaufray et al., eds., *Le Fayoum: Archéologie – Histoire – Religion.* Wiesbaden: Harrassowitz, pp. 101–128.

Pries, A. (2022). *Traditio obligat – Variatio delectat. Zur Überlieferungsdynamik altägyptischer Traditionsliteratur.* Ägyptologische Abhandlungen 83. Wiesbaden: Harrassowitz.

Quack, J. F. (1994). *Die Lehren des Ani: ein neuägyptischer Weisheitstext in seinem kulturellen Umfeld*. Orbis biblicus et orientalis 141. Freiburg: Universitätsverlag.

Quack, J. F. (1999a). Review of P. Gallo, *Ostraca demotici e ieratici*. Enchoria, 25, 192–196.

Quack, J. F. (1999b). A New Bilingual Fragment from the British Museum (Papyrus BM EA 69574. *Journal of Egyptian Archaeology*, 55, 153–164.

Quack, J. F. (2002). Die Dienstanweisung des Oberlehrers aus dem Buch vom Tempel. In H. Beinlich et al., eds., *5. Ägyptologische Tempeltagung: Würzburg, 23–26 September 1999*. Wiesbaden: Harrassowitz, pp. 159–171.

Quack, J. F. (2006). Die hieratischen und hieroglyphischen Texte aus Tebtynis – Ein Überblick. In K. Ryholt, ed., *The Carlsberg Papyri 7. Hieratic Texts from the Collection*. Carsten Niebuhr Institute Publications 30. Copenhagen: Museum Tusculanum Press, pp. 1–7.

Quack, J. F. (2010a). Egyptian Writing for Non-Egyptian Languages and Vice Versa: A Short Overview. In A. de Voogt and I. L. Finkel, eds., *The Idea of Writing: Play and Complexity*. Leiden: Brill, pp. 317–325.

Quack, J. F. (2010b). Difficult Hieroglyphs and Unreadable Demotic? How the Ancient Egyptians Dealt with the Complexities of Their Script. In A. de Voogt and I. L. Finke, eds., *The Idea of Writing: Play and Complexity*. Leiden: Brill, pp. 235–251.

Quack, J. F. (2011). Textedition, Texterschließung, Textinterpretation. In A. Verbovsek, C. Jones, and B. Backes, eds., *Methodik und Didaktik in der Ägyptologie: Herausforderungen eines kulturwissenschaftlichen Paradigmewechsels in den Altertumswissenschaften*. Ägyptologie und Kulturwissenschaft 4. Paderborn: Wilhelm Fink, pp. 533–549.

Quack, J. F. (2015). Rohrfedertorheiten? Bemerkungen zum römerzeitlichen Hieratisch. In U. Verhoeven, ed., *Ägyptologische "Binsen"-Weisheiten I–II: Neue Forschungen und Methoden der Hieratistik, Akten zweier Tagungen in Mainz im April 2011 und März 2013*. Einzelveröffentlichungen 14. Mainz: Akademie der Wissenschaften und der Literatur/Stuttgart: Franz Steiner Verlag, pp. 435–469.

Quack, J. F. (2016a). The Last Stand? What Remains Egyptian in Oxyrhynchus. In K. Ryholt and G. Barjamovic, eds., *Problems of Canonicity and Identity Formation in Ancient Egypt and Mesopotamia*. CNI Publications 43. Copenhagen: Museum Tusculanum Press, pp. 105–126.

Quack, J. F. (2016b). Wie normativ ist das Buch vom Tempel, und wann und wo ist es so? In M. Ullmann, ed., *10. Ägyptologische Tempeltagung: Ägyptische Tempel zwischen Normierung und Individualität. München, 29–31 August 2014*. Königtum, Staat und Gesellschaft früher Hochkulturen 3,5. Wiesbaden: Harrassowitz, pp. 99–109.

Quack, J. F. (2017a). On the Regionalization of Roman-Period Egyptian Hands. In J. Cromwell and E. Grossman, eds., *Scribal Repertoires in Egypt from the New Kingdom to the Early Islamic Period*. Oxford: Oxford University Press, pp. 184–210.

Quack, J. F. (2017b). How the Coptic Script Came About. In E. Grossman et al., eds., *Greek Influence on Egyptian-Coptic: Contact-induced Change in an Ancient African Language*. Lingua Aegyptia Studia Monographia 17. Hamburg: Widmaier Verlag, pp. 27–96.

Quack, J. F. (2019). Demotische Verwaltungstexte in hieratischer Schrift. In K.-Th. Zauzich, ed., *Akten der 8. Internationalen Konferenz für Demotische Studien*. Wiesbaden: Harrassowitz, pp. 145–157.

Quack, J. F. (2020a). Eine spätzeitliche Handschrift der Lehre des Cheti (Papyrus Berlin P 14423). In Sh.-W. Hsu, J. Moje, and V. P.-M. Laisney, eds., *Ein Kundiger, der in die Gottesworte eingedrungen ist. Festschrift für den Ägyptologen Karl Jansen-Winkeln zum 65. Geburtstag*. Münster: Zaphon, pp. 233–251.

Quack, J. F. (2020b). Zwei demotische Briefe in hieratischer Schrift. In K. Ryholt, ed., *The Carlsberg Papyri 15: Hieratic Texts from Tebtunis Including a Survey of Illustrated Papyri*. Carsten Niebuhr Publications 45. Copenhagen: Museum Tusculanum Press, pp. 141–149.

Quack, J. F. (2020c). Eine Liste von Formen des Mond-Thot. In K. Ryholt, ed., *The Carlsberg Papyri 15: Hieratic Texts from Tebtunis Including a Survey of Illustrated Papyri*. Carsten Niebuhr Publications 45. Copenhagen: Museum Tusculanum Press, pp. 19–24.

Quack, J. F. (2020d). Ein alphabetisch sortiertes Handbuch der Hieroglyphenzeichen. In K. Ryholt, ed., *The Carlsberg Papyri 15: Hieratic Texts from Tebtunis Including a Survey of Illustrated Papyri*. Carsten Niebuhr Publications 45. Copenhagen: Museum Tusculanum Press, pp. 77–106.

Quack, J. F. (2021). Priestly Scholars in Late Egypt: The Theoretical Side. *Journal of Ancient Near Eastern History,* 8, 73–90.

Quack, J. F. (2022). Klassisch-ägyptische Texte in späthieratischem Gewande. *Zeitschrift für Ägyptische Sprache und Altertumskunde,* 149, 91–105.

Quack, J. F. (2023a). The Egyptian Classification of Hieroglyphs. In S. Polis, ed., *Guide to the Writing Systems of Ancient Egypt*. Cairo: Institut français d'archéologie orientale, pp. 140–143.

Quack, J. F. (2023b). Magischer Text (Demotisch in hieratischer Schrift). Papyrus Leiden Pap. Inst. P. 1000. In F. A. J. Hoogendijk and J. V. Stolk, eds., *Greek, Hieratic, Demotic and Coptic Papyri and Ostraca in the Leiden Papyrological Institute*. Papyrologica Lugduno-Batava 40. Leiden: Brill, pp. 5–12.

Quack, J. F. (2023c). Modellbriefe als Mittel des Schreiberausbildung im Alten Ägypten. In S. Deichert, M. Elnoubi, S. M. Abdel Moaty, and H. Wilde, eds., *Modelle im Alten Ägypten. Objekte der Wissens*. Berlin: Kulturverlag Kadmos, pp. 79–149.

Ragab, M. (2024). *The Workmen's Graffiti in the Valley of the Kings*. Uppsala Studies in Egyptology 7. Uppsala: Uppsala Universitet.

Ragazzoli, C. (2016). Genres textuels et supports matériels: une inscription de visiteur comme exercice sur ostracon (Ostracon University College 31918). *NeHeT, revue numérique d'égyptologie*, 4, 65–76.

Ragazzoli, C. (2017a). *La grotte des scribes à Deir el-Bahari: la tombe MMA 504 et ses graffiti*. Mémoires publiés par les membres de l'Institut français d'archéologie orientale 135. Cairo: Institut français d'archéologie orientale.

Ragazzoli, C. (2017b). Beyond Authors and Copyists: The Role of Variation in Ancient Egyptian and New Kingdom Literary Production. In T. Gillen, ed., *(Re)productive Traditions in Ancient Egypt*. Aegyptiaca Leodensia 10. Liège: Presses Universitaires de Liège, pp. 95–126.

Ragazzoli, C. (2019). *Scribes: Les artisans du texte de l'Égypte ancienne (1550–1000)*. Paris: Les Belles Lettres.

Ragazzoli, C., Hassan, Kh., & Salvador, C., eds. (2023). *Graffiti and Rock Inscriptions from Ancient Egypt: A Companion to Secondary Epigraphy*. Bibliothèque d'Étude 182. Cairo: Institut français d'archéologie orientale.

Ragazzoli, C. & Albert, F., eds. (2025). *Questions sur la scripturalité égyptienne. Des registres graphiques aux espaces d'écriture*. Bibliothèque d'Étude 192. Cairo: Institut français d'archéologie orientale.

Regulski, I. (2009). The Beginning of Hieratic Writing in Egypt. *Studien zur Altägyptischen Kultur*, 38, 259–274.

Regulski, I. (2010). *A Palaeographic Study of Early Writing in Egypt*. Orientalia Lovaniensia Analecta 195. Leuven: Peeters.

Ryholt, K. (2005). On the Contents and Nature of the Tebtunis Temple Library. A Status Report. In S. Lippert and M. Schentuleit, eds., *Tebtynis und Soknopaiou Nesos. Leben im römerzeitlichen Fajum*. Wiesbaden: Harrassowitz, pp. 141–170.

Ryholt, K. (2018). Scribal Habits at the Tebtunis Temple Library: On Materiality, Formal Features, and Palaeography. In J. Cromwell and E. Grossman, eds., *Scribal Repertoires in Egypt from the New Kingdom to the Early Islamic Period*. Oxford: Oxford University Press, pp. 153–183.

Ryholt, K. (2020a). ed., *The Carlsberg Papyri 15: Hieratic Texts from Tebtunis Including a Survey of Illustrated Papyri*. With contributions by A. Kucharek, D. Petrova, A. H. Pries, J. F. Quack, K. Ryholt, S. Töpfer. Carsten Niebuhr Institute Publications 45. Copenhagen: Museum Tusculanum Press.

Ryholt, K. (2020b). Demotic Documents with Hieratic Imperial Titulary. In K. Ryholt, ed., *The Carlsberg Papyri 15: Hieratic Texts from Tebtunis Including a Survey of Illustrated Papyri*. Carsten Niebuhr Institute Publications 45. Copenhagen: Museum Tusculanum Press, pp. 151–164.

Sauneron, S. (1959). *Catalogue des ostraca hiératiques non littéraires de Deir el-Médineh (nos 550 à 623)*. Documents de Fouilles de l'Institut français d'archéologie orientale 13. Cairo: Institut français d'archéologie orientale.

Scalf, F. & Flannery, A. (2019). Printing God's Words with the Devil's Infernal Machine. *News & Notes Quarterly Newsletter*, 242, 18–24.

Schenkel, W. (2012). Die Entzifferung der Hieroglyphen und Karl Lepsius. In V. M. Lepper and I. Hafemann, eds., *Karl Richard Lepsius. Der Begründer des deutschen Ägyptologie*. Kaleidogramme 90. Berlin: Kulturverlag Kadmos, pp. 37–78.

Schneider, T. (2023). *Language Contact in Ancient Egypt*. Einführungen und Quellentexte zur Ägyptologie 16. Berlin: LIT Verlag.

Sethe, K. (1924). *Ägyptische Lesestücke zum Gebrauch im akademischen Unterricht*. Leipzig: J. C. Hinrichs.

Shaw, I. (2000), ed. *The Oxford History of Ancient Egypt*. Oxford: Oxford University Press.

Shisha-Halevy, A. (1978). An Early North-West Semitic Text in the Egyptian Hieratic Script. *Orientalia*, 47, 145–162.

Silvestri, J. P. (2023). The Oldest Berber Text(s)? Egyptian Evidence for the Ancient Libyan Language(s). *Études et Documents Berbères*, 49–50, 319–348.

Simpson, W. K. (2003). *The Literature of Ancient Egypt*. New Haven: Yale University Press.

Smith, H. & Smith, A. (1976). A Reconsideration of the Kamose Texts. *Zeitschrift für Ägyptische Sprache und Altertumskunde,* 103, 48–76.

Spalinger, A. (2002). *The Transformation of an Ancient Egyptian Narrative: P. Sallier III and the Battle of Kadesh*. Göttinger Orientforschungen 4, Reihe: Ägypten 40. Wiesbaden: Harrassowitz.

Stadler, M. A. (2008). On the Demise of Egyptian Writing: Working with a Problematic Source Basis. In J. Baines, J. Bennet, and S. Houston, eds., *The Disappearance of Writing Systems: Perspectives on Literacy and Communication*. London: Equinox Publishing, pp. 157–181.

Stauder, A. (2013). *Linguistic Dating of Middle Egyptian Literary Texts*. Linguae Aegyptiae Studia Monographica 12. Hamburg: Widmaier Verlag.

Stauder, A. (2020). La forme poétique de l'*Enseignement de Sehetepibré*. In K. Gabler et al., eds., *Text-Bild-Objekte im archäeologischen Kontext: Festschrift für Susanne Bickel*. Linguae Aegyptia Studia Monographica 22. Hamburg: Widmaier Verlag, pp. 239–256.

Sweeney, D. (1998). Friendship and Frustration: A Study in Papyri Deir el-Medina IV–VI. *Journal of Egyptian Archaeology,* 84, 101–122.

Tabin, J. A. (2023). Optical Character Recognition Applied to Hieratic. Hieratic Studies Online 5, Mainz. http://doi.org/10.25358/openscience-9590.

Tacke, N. (2001). *Verspunkte als Gliederungsmittel in ramessidischen Schülerhandschriften*. Studien zur Archäologie und Geschichte Altägyptens 22. Heidelberg: Heidelberger Orientverlag.

Tallet, P. (2005). Un nouveau témoin des "Devoirs du vizir" dans la tombe d'Aménémopé (Thèbes, TT 29). *Chronique d'Égypte*, 80(159–160), 66–75.

Tallet, P. (2010). La fin des Devoirs du vizir. In E. Warmenbol and V. Angenot, eds., *Thèbes aux 101 portes: mélanges à la mémoire de Roland Tefnin*. Turnhout: Brepols/Association Égyptologique Reine Élisabeth, pp. 153–163.

Uljas, S. (2013). Linguistic Consciousness. In J. Stauder-Prochet, A. Stauder and W. Wendrich, eds., *UCLA Encyclopedia of Egyptology*. Los Angeles. https://escholarship.org/uc/item/0rb1k58f

Unter, S. (2025). *Multimodal Analysis and Retrieval for Fragmentary Historical Documents with Machine Learning: A Case Study on Ancient Egyptian Hieratic Papyri*, PhD Dissertation, University of Basel.

Vandorpe, K. & Verreth, H. (2012). Temple of Narmouthis: House of the Ostraca. In the Trismegistos database. Available online at https://www.trismegistos.org/arch/archives/pdf/534.pdf. Accessed 26 September 2024.

Varille, A. (1968). *Inscriptions concernant l'architecte Amenhotep fils de Hapou*. Bibliothèque d'étude 44. Cairo: Institut français d'archéologie orientale.

Venturini, I. (2007). *Recherches sur les exercises scolaires sur ostraca et tablettes hiéroglyphique et hiératiques dans l'Égypte pharaonique*, 3 vols. Unpublished PhD thesis, Université Montpellier III.

Verhoeven, U. (2001). *Untersuchungen zur späthieratischen Buchschrift*. Orientalia Lovaniensia Analecta 99. Leuven: Peeters.

Verhoeven, U. (2015). Stand und Aufgaben der Erforschung des Hieratischen und der Kursivhieroglyphen. In U. Verhoeven, ed., *Ägyptologische "Binsen"-Weisheiten I–II: Neue Forschungen und Methoden der Hieratistik, Akten zweier Tagungen in Mainz im April 2011 und März 2013*. Einzelveröffentlichungen 14. Mainz: Akademie der Wissenschaften und der Literatur/Stuttgart: Franz Steiner Verlag, pp. 23–63.

Verhoeven, U. (2019). Georg Möller (1876–1921): Spuren und Wahrnehmungen. In M. Brose et al., eds., *En détail: Philologie und Archäologie im Diskurs: Festschrift für Hans-Werner Fischer-Elfert*. Zeitschrift für Ägyptische Sprache und Altertumskunde Beiheft 7. Berlin: De Gruyte, pp. 1159–1176.

Verhoeven, U. (2020a). Paratextual Signs in Egyptian Funerary and Religious Texts from the Saite and Early Ptolemaic Period. In N. Carlig et al., eds., *Signes dans les textes: Continuités et ruptures des pratiques scribales en Égypte pharaonique, gréco-romaine et byzantine*. Papyrologica Leodiensia 9. Liège: Presses Universitaires de Liège, pp. 95–112.

Verhoeven, U. (2020b). *Dipinti von Besuchern des Grabes N13.1 in Assiut*, 2 vols. The Asyut Project 15. Wiesbaden: Harrassowitz.

Verhoeven, U. (2023a). Hieratic. In A. Stauder and W. Wendrich, eds., *UCLA Encyclopedia of Egyptology*. Los Angeles. https://escholarship.org/uc/item/1fh2r94g.

Verhoeven, U. (2023b). A Step Back into the Past: New Kingdom Scribal Activities in the Necropolis of Asyut. In C. Ragazzoli, Kh. Hassan, and C. Salvador, eds., *Graffiti and Rock Inscriptions from Ancient Egypt: A Companion to Secondary Epigraphy*. Bibliothèque d'Étude 182. Cairo: Institut français d'archéologie orientale, pp. 239–253.

Verhoeven, U. (2023c). Writing Book of the Dead Manuscripts: Tasks and Traditions. In R. Lucarelli and M. A. Stadler, eds., *The Oxford Handbook of the Egyptian Book of the Dead*. Oxford: Oxford University Press, pp. 76–115.

Vernus, P. (1990). Les espaces de l'écrit dans l'Égypte pharaonique. *Bulletin de la Societé Française d'Égyptologie*, 119, 35–56.

Virey, Ph. (1887). Étude sur un parchemin rapporté des Thébes. *Mémoires publiés par les membres de la Mission archéologique français au Caire*, I.3. Paris: Libraire de la Societé asiatique.

Vleeming, S. (1991). Review of A. Gasse, *Données nouvelles (1988)*. *Enchoria*, 18, 217–227.

Weber, M. (1959). *Beiträge zur Kenntnis des Schrift- und Buchwesens der alten Ägypter*, Unpublished PhD Dissertation, University of Cologne.

Wente, E. F. (1967). *Late Ramesside Letters*. Studies in Ancient Oriental Civilization 33. Chicago: University of Chicago Press.

Wente, E. F. (1990). *Letters from Ancient Egypt*. Writings from the Ancient World 1. Atlanta: Scholars Press.

Wente, E. F. (2001). Scripts: Hieratic. In D. Redford, ed., *The Oxford Encyclopedia of Ancient Egypt*, vol. 3. New York: Oxford University Press/Cairo: The American University in Cairo Press, pp. 206–210.

Willems, H. (2023). Zu den eingekerbten hieratischen Zeichen auf Särgen des Mittleren Reiches aus Dayr al-Barsha. In S. Gerhards et al., eds., *Schöne Denkmäler sind entstanden: Studien zu Ehren von Ursula Verhoeven*. Heidelberg: Propylaeum, pp. 611–620.

Wimmer, S. (1995). *Hieratische Paläographie der nicht-literarischen Ostraka der 19. und 20. Dynastie*, 2 vols. Ägypten und Altes Testament 28. Wiesbaden: Harrassowitz.

Wimmer, S. (2001). Palaeography and the Dating of Ramesside Ostraca. *Lingua Aegyptia*, 9, 285–292.

Wimmer, S. (2008). *Palästinisches Hieratisch: Die Zahl- und Sonderzeichen in der althebräischen Schrift*. Ägypten und Altes Testament 75. Wiesbaden: Harrassowitz.

Wimmer, S. (2018). Palestinian Hieratic in Non-Hebrew Context: Egyptian Numerals and Special Signs in Regions Neighboring Israel. In I. Shai et al., eds., *Tell It in Gath: Studies in the History and Archaeology of Israel; Essays in Honor of Aren M. Maeir on the Occasion of His Sixtieth Birthday*. Ägypten und Altes Testament 90. Münster: Zaphon, pp. 709–721.

Winand, J. (1998). La pontuaction avant la ponctuation: L'organisation du message écrit dans l'Égypte pharaonique. In J.-M. Defays, L. Rosier, and F. Tilkin, eds., *Á qui appartient la ponctuation? Actes du colloque international et interdisciplinaire de Liège (13–15 mars 1997)*. Paris: Duculot, pp. 163–177.

Winand, J. (2020a). When Classical Authors Encountered Egyptian Epigraphy. In V. Davies and D. Laboury, eds., *The Oxford Handbook of Egyptian Epigraphy and Palaeography*. Oxford: Oxford University Press, pp. 163–175.

Winand, J. (2020b). Quand le texte ne suffit plus. Éléments de réflexion sur la notion de paratexte dans l'Égypte ancienne. In N. Carlig et al., eds., *Signes dans les textes: Continuités et ruptures des pratiques scribales en Égypte pharaonique, gréco-romaine et byzantine*. Papyrologica Leodiensia 9. Liège: Presses Universitaires de Liège, pp. 11–40.

Winand, J. (2021). Les hièroglyphes égyptiens après Kircher: la naissance de la philologie orientale au XVIIIe siècle. In C. Bonnet, J.-Fr. Courouau, and E. Dieu, eds., *Lux Philologiæ, L'essor de la philologie au XVIIIe siècle*. Geneva: Droz, pp. 277–326.

Acknowledgements

With any synthesis of a topic there is an unavoidable overlap with existing literature in the field, and this is also true of this Element. Although the work of others can be partly traced through the bibliographical references, the restrictions of the format meant that I could not always be as inclusive as I might have wished. The focus has been on recent publications with a direct bearing on the arguments, but interested readers should be able to find further literature through the references cited, including older but still very much relevant contributions. For accessibility all citations have been translated into English; my apologies to colleagues, whose original formulations are in every case more elegant than my translations of them.

Even a synthesis represents a personal take on a subject, and I have particularly drawn on material from those periods that I have worked with myself; it goes without saying that others would no doubt have done this very differently. If this Element complements previous work, it probably does so primarily in its structure and its discussion of methodological issues. It is also brief, and in English, which may attract a different audience than many other works available (see Section 6.1). Some of the more recent surveys of hieratic were explicitly conceived of as material for graduate classes in Egyptology, which is rather different from this one. My aim has not been to write a teaching volume, even if students of hieratic may find something of interest in it, but rather something aimed at nonspecialists who may be curious about this less familiar Egyptian script, its use, and its cultural context.

I am happy to express my gratitude to a number of people who were involved in the production of this volume in the Elements series. Andréas Stauder originally suggested the topic to me and provided feedback during the writing process. Stéphane Polis very kindly read a draft and made several useful comments which did much to improve it; I am particularly thankful to him for having spent time scrupulously checking details and making substantive suggestions for improvements. Joachim F. Quack provided useful input on O. Narmouthis 35 (Figure 23). My thanks are also due to my student assistant, Julie Schwartzlose Christensen, who formatted and checked the references, thereby saving me a lot of work during an exceptionally busy term. Finally, the volume benefited from a number of insightful comments from two anonymous peer reviewers who were both thorough and constructive, and I am grateful to them both for having spent their precious research time on it. Naturally any remaining mistakes are entirely mine.

One last acknowledgement is due to my old supervisor, John Ray, who is partly responsible for putting me on the path that led here: his suggestion when I first arrived in his office many years ago as a graduate student, delivered with his with usual understatement, was that I should simply sit down by myself and learn hieratic ('It can be good to know'). I am glad I took his advice.

Cambridge Elements

Writing in the Ancient World

Andréas Stauder
École Pratique des Hautes Études–PSL (EPHE)

Andréas Stauder is Professor of Egyptology at the École Pratique des Hautes Études–PSL, in Paris. His research focusses on the origins and early development of writing in Egypt and in comparative perspective, the visual aesthetics and semiotics of Egyptian hieroglyphic writing, the historical linguistics of the Egyptian-Coptic language, the poetics of ancient Egyptian literature, and Egyptian inscriptions in space.

Editorial Board

Wolfgang Behr, *University of Zürich*
Silvia Ferrara, *University of Bologna*
Stephen Houston, *Brown University*
Philip Huyse, *École Pratique des Hautes Études–PSL, Paris*
Cale Johnson, *Freie Universität, Berlin*
David Lurie, *Columbia University*
Rachel Mairs, *University of Reading*
Ingo Strauch, *University of Lausanne*

About the Series

The study of ancient writing, though not an institutionalised field itself, has developed over the past two decades into a dynamic domain of inquiry across specialisms. The series aims to reflect and contribute to this ongoing interdisciplinary dialogue while challenging schematic views on writing in the ancient world. Written by a team of specialists, volumes in the series will be broadly accessible to students and scholars.

Cambridge Elements

Writing in the Ancient World

Elements in the Series

Cypro-Minoan and Its Writers: At Home and Overseas
Cassandra M. Donnelly

Writing in Bronze Age Crete: 'Minoan' Linear A
Ester Salgarella

Hieratic: An Ancient Egyptian Cursive Script
Fredrik Hagen

A full series listing is available at: www.cambridge.org/EWAW

For EU product safety concerns, contact us at Calle de José Abascal, 56–1°, 28003 Madrid, Spain or eugpsr@cambridge.org.